Mrs. Dalloway

Mapping Streams of Consciousness

Twayne's Masterwork Studies

Robert Lecker, General Editor

Mrs. Dalloway

Mapping Streams of Consciousness

✳

DAVID DOWLING

TWAYNE PUBLISHERS • BOSTON
A Division of G. K. Hall & Co.

Twayne's Masterwork Studies No. 67

Copyright 1991 by G. K. Hall & Co.
All rights reserved.
Published by Twayne Publishers
A division of G. K. Hall & Co.
70 Lincoln Street
Boston, Massachusetts 02111

Copyediting supervised by Barbara Sutton.
Book production by Janet Z. Reynolds.
Typeset by Huron Valley Graphics, Ann Arbor, Michigan.

10 9 8 7 6 5 4 3 2 1 (hc)
10 9 8 7 6 5 4 3 2 1 (pb)

The paper used in this publication meets the minimum requirements
of American National Standard for Information Sciences—Permanence
of Paper for Printed Library Materials, ANSI Z39.48-1984.⊚™

Printed and bound in the United States of America.

Library of Congress Cataloging-in-Publication Data

Dowling, David.
    Mrs. Dalloway : mapping streams of consciousness / David Dowling.
       p.   cm.—(Twayne's masterwork studies ; no. 67)
    Includes bibliographical references and index.
    ISBN 0-8057-9414-X (alk. paper).—ISBN 0-8057-8145-5 (pbk. :
alk. paper)
    1. Woolf, Virginia, 1882–1941. Mrs. Dalloway. 2. Stream of
consciousness fiction. I. Title. II. Series.
PR6045.O72M735 1991
823'.912—dc20   90-48715

To Shawna, encore

The clock of St Margaret's was saying two minutes later than Big Ben that it was half past eleven. But her voice was a woman's voice, since it is impossible to have anything to do with inanimate objects without giving them sex. . . . [It] spoke as a woman speaks. There was a vibration in the core of the sound so that each word, or note, comes fluttering, alive, yet with some reluctance to inflict its vitality, some grief for the past which holds it back, some impulse nevertheless to glide into the recesses of the heart and there bury itself in ring after ring of sound, so that Mr Walsh, as he walked past St Margaret's, and heard the bells toll the half hour felt. . .

—"The Hours," 27 June 1923,
The Virginia Woolf Manuscripts from the Monk's House Papers at the University of Sussex

the power which adds the supreme flavor to existence—the power of taking hold of experience, of turning it round, slowly in the light.

—*Mrs. Dalloway*

Contents

Note on the References
and Acknowledgments

Page references in this study are to the Penguin Modern Classics edition, first published in 1964. The publishing history of *Mrs. Dalloway* is complicated because Leonard Woolf obtained simultaneous publication of the novel in English (Hogarth Press) and American (Harcourt, Brace & Co.) editions, on 14 May 1925. This arrangement necessitated working simultaneously from proofed typescripts and resulted inevitably in some variations.

Because *Mrs. Dalloway* is not divided into chapters, the gaps dividing sections are important. The Harcourt edition lacks space divisions at the following four points: after "foo swee too eem oo" (92); "Dr. Holmes, looking not quite so kind" (104); "So that was Dr. Holmes" (167); and "And she came in from the little room" (206). In all cases, Virginia Woolf wished these divisions (eleven in Hogarth, seven in Harcourt) to be indicated by two blank lines.

Of the textual changes, many are minor but one is worth noting. Harcourt adds a sentence at the end of Clarissa's scene alone at the party, which clarifies the effect of Septimus's death on Clarissa. After "The leaden circles dissolved in the air," the American edition reads, "He made her feel the beauty, made her feel the fun."

After comparing the British and American editions, E. F. Shields, in "The American Edition of *Mrs. Dalloway*" (*Studies in Bibliography* 27 [1974]: 157–75), concludes, "We have two versions—both of which can legitimately claim to be authoritative first editions." This study works from the British edition, specifically the fourth English edition published by Penguin in association with the Hogarth Press in 1964.

Virginia Woolf, age forty-five, photographed by Man Ray. Used by permission of Chatto & Windus and the Hogarth Press.

Chronology:
Virginia Woolf's Life and Works

1882	Virginia Stephen is born on 25 January in London, to Leslie Stephen and Julia Duckworth Stephen.
1895	Mother Julia dies, and Virginia becomes mentally ill.
1897	Attends Greek and history classes at King's College, London; her half-sister Stella marries, becomes pregnant, and dies.
1899	Older brother Thoby Stephen enters Trinity College, Cambridge.
1902	Father becomes Sir Leslie Stephen.
1904	Publishes her first review. Her father dies, and she has a second breakdown. The family moves to 46 Gordon Square, Bloomsbury, London.
1905	Teaches at Morley College, London.
1906	Brother Thoby Stephen dies of typhoid.
1907	Sister Vanessa marries Clive Bell, art critic.
1910	Is involved in the "*Dreadnought* Hoax" and does volunteer work for women's suffrage. The First Post-Impressionist Exhibition is organized by her friend Roger Fry.
1912	Marries Leonard Woolf.
1913	Suffers mental illness and attempts suicide.
1914	World War begins in July.
1915	The Woolfs move to Richmond on the outskirts of London, and *The Voyage Out* (featuring Mr. and Mrs. Dalloway) is published.
1917	Experiences the German bombing of London in December. Leonard Woolf sets up the Hogarth Press as a way to keep Virginia occupied at times of mental stress, and publishes Katherine Mansfield (in 1918) and T. S. Eliot (in 1919), as well as Woolf herself; the Woolfs refuse Joyce's *Ulysses*.

1918	World War I ends in November.
1918–1919	Spanish influenza epidemic.
1919	The Woolfs move to Sussex. *Night and Day* is published; also *Eminent Victorians,* by Virginia's friend Lytton Strachey, the *The Economic Consequences of Peace,* by Maynard Keynes, correctly foreseeing a second world war if reparations against Germany are too punitive.
1921	*Monday or Tuesday,* a collection of short stories, is published by the Hogarth Press. Is ill for four months.
1922	*Jacob's Room* is published; in October an old family friend, Kitty Maxse, dies, and Virginia begins to enlarge her story "Mrs. Dalloway in Bond Street" into a novel. Reads Joyce and Proust.
1923	Works on *Mrs. Dalloway,* introducing Peter Walsh. "Mrs. Dalloway in Bond Street" appears in the *Dial* in July. The Hogarth Press publishes T. S. Eliot's *The Waste Land.* A coalition of Labour and Liberals wins the general election.
1924	The Woolfs move back into London, to 52 Tavistock Square, Bloomsbury, and Virginia begins rewriting *Mrs. Dalloway.* Completes it on 9 October. The Conservatives beat Labour in a general election.
1925	*Mrs. Dalloway* is published on 14 May; *The Common Reader,* a collection of essays, is also published. Is ill for three months.
1926	The General Strike in Britain lasts nine days.
1927	*To the Lighthouse* is published.
1928	Writes an introduction for the American edition of *Mrs. Dalloway. Orlando,* a fantastical biography, is published.
1929	*A Room of One's Own,* a feminist essay, is published.
1931	*The Waves* is published.
1937	*The Years* is published.
1938	*Three Guineas,* another collection of feminist essays, is published.
1939	World War II breaks out, and the Woolfs are on Hitler's death list.
1940	*Roger Fry: A Biography,* is published.
1941	Commits suicide by drowning in the River Ouse. *Between the Acts* is published posthumously.

Literary and
Historical Context

*

Virginia Woolf in her mother's Victorian dress, May 1926. Photograph by Marianne Beck, *Vogue*. Used by permission.

1

Bloomsbury, War, and Modernism

Virginia Woolf was eighteen at the turn of the century. She grew up in the solid comfort and conformity of a bourgeois London family in the Victorian age. What jolted Woolf from the intellectual and emotional deadening of her society was not the untimely deaths of her parents, her brother, and her half-sister, or even the changing world around her, but her involvement in the so-called Bloomsbury group.

This loosely knit circle of university and artist friends of Virginia's brother Thoby gathered around the Stephen household when she was in her twenties, in about 1904. The Bloomsbury group included novelist E. M. Forster, economist John Maynard Keynes, artists Duncan Grant and Virginia's sister Vanessa Bell, essayist Lytton Strachey, and art critics Clive Bell and Roger Fry. Most of the group members came from the middle and upper-middle professional classes, and their families often had links with well-known nineteenth-century families of artists and social thinkers, such as the Huxleys and Paxtons. The group members shared a general admiration for the philosopher G. E. Moore, who taught many of the men in the group at Cambridge University. They admired especially a statement in Moore's philosophical work *Principia Ethica:* "By far the most valuable things which we know or can imagine are certain states of consciousness, which may roughly be described as the pleasures of human intercourse and the enjoyment of beautiful objects." The enjoyment of good company and good art became the aim of the Bloomsbury group.

The circle's artistic principles were epitomized in the First Post-Impressionist Exhibition of art, organized by Roger Fry in 1910. This landmark showing introduced to a reluctant British public such Continental painters as Matisse, Manet, Picasso, van Gogh, Gauguin, and Cézanne. The catchphrase that became associated with the Bloomsbury group's aesthetic sense was "significant form," suggesting the importance of design and composition in all artistic works, whether plastic, painterly or literary. Fry and his friend Clive Bell (who became Virginia's brother-in-law) argued that the postimpressionist painters displayed a strong sense of significant form.

Another appeal of these painters lay in their subject matter, which was often pacific—bathers, still lifes, landscapes, the interiors of rooms. When the Great War broke out, the Bloomsbury group achieved notoriety for its pacifism. Group members had shared a cynical distrust of the military for a long time, demonstrating it in the "*Dreadnought* Hoax" of 1910, when they successfully infiltrated the Royal Navy, disguised as an Abyssinian delegation (with Woolf herself in robes and blackface).

The group's stand for a new art attracted the antagonism of most of England. Even more so did its stand for a new morality, particularly for open acceptance of homosexuality (E. M. Forster and Lytton Strachey were homosexual, the latter flamboyantly so). The ruling class, the politicians, and the masses all saw Woolf and her friends as upper-middle-class dandies haughtily enjoying their privileged ease. But the truth is that they were not at all "counterculture" in a faddish sense. Several members worked long and hard for political change, particularly Leonard Woolf and Maynard Keynes. Indeed, the group's activities between 1923 and 1925 (when most of *Mrs. Dalloway* was composed) show a remarkable range of accomplishments. The following books were published: by Clive Bell, *On British Freedom* and *The Legend of Monte della Sibilla* (illustrated by Vanessa Bell and Duncan

Grant); by Roger Fry, *Duncan Grant, A Sampler of Castile,* and *The Artist and Psycho-analysis;* by E. M. Forster, *Pharos and Pharillon, A Passage to India,* and *Anonymity;* by J. M. Keynes, *A Tract of Monetary Reform, The Economic Consequences of Mr. Churchill,* and *A Short View of Russia;* by Leonard Woolf, *Fabian Essays on Co-operation* (editor) and *Fear and Politics;* by Mary MacCarthy, *A Nineteenth Century Childhood;* by Virginia Woolf, "Mr Bennett and Mrs Brown," *The Common Reader,* and *Mrs. Dalloway.* As well, the Woolfs' Hogarth Press began to publish Sigmund Freud's *Collected Papers* and *The Psycho-analytic Library* and T. S. Eliot's *The Waste Land.* While Lytton Strachey lectured on Pope at Cambridge, Keynes became chairman of the board of *The Nation and Atheneum* magazine, and Leonard Woolf became its literary editor.

Living in such a vigorous and eclectic environment, Virginia Woolf would have had a precise, practical knowledge of the political and economic issues facing England, the British Empire, and the world in the early part of the twentieth century. In addition, her own mental illness and Hogarth Press's part in introducing Freud's writing into English gave her an unusually intimate and advanced understanding of theories about the mind and mental disorders.

The Great War provided Virginia Woolf with a symbolic focus and preoccupied her from the time of *Jacob's Room* to that of her last novel, *Between the Acts,* in which another world war looms. For example, she wrote to the *Times* about a phenomenon she observed while staying near Lewes, Sussex, in August 1916. She noted that the gunfire in France "sounds like the beating of gigantic carpets by gigantic women, at a distance. You may almost see them holding the carpets in their strong arms by the four corners, tossing them into the air, and bringing them down with a thud while the dust rises in a cloud about their heads. All walks on the Downs this summer are accompanied by this sinister sound of far-off beating, which is sometimes as faint as the ghost of an echo, and sometimes rises almost from the next fold of grey land."[1] Her concern was how the ordinary person could relate to such vast events, how "the desire to be somehow impossibly, and therefore all the more mysteriously, concerned in secret affairs of national importance is very strong at the present moment." She was fascinated by the contradictions of the time, and by the way daily life continued in the midst of carnage. For example, one of the superstitions she encountered in Sussex was a belief that the cloudy weather was in keeping with wartime. Unfortunately, she observed, "the sun has shone fiercely since then and is shining still."[2]

What Woolf could not guess about the war from the sounds on Sussex downs or in the streets of London she could find vividly expressed in poetry. She may have read Wilfred Owen's poem "Mental Cases" ("These are men whose minds the Dead have ravished") or perhaps Edmund Blunden's "1916 seen from 1921":

> and I
> Dead as the men I loved, wait while life drags
> Its wounded length from those sad streets of war
> Into green places here, that were my own;
> But now what once was mine is mine no more,
> I seek such neighbors here and I find none.

She had herself lived through a bombing of London in 1917, and the following year observed in her diary, "The more one sees of the effects on young men who should be happy the more one detests the whole thing."[3] In that same year she watched her brother talking with a German prisoner, and she reasoned that the experience of war must involve a repression of the imagination: "The existence of life in another human being is as difficult to realize as a play of Shakespeare when the book is shut. This occurred to me when I saw Adrian talking to the tall German prisoner. By right they should have been killing each other. The reason why it is easy to kill another person must be that one's imagination is too sluggish to conceive what his life means to him—the infinite possibilities of a succession of days which are furled in him, and have already been spent."[4]

Only a few people—like Clarissa Dalloway—have the imaginative capacity to conceive of a life separate from their own, and so to become truly pacifist. The majority lack imagination and fall back into old ways and generalizations. Woolf was shocked by the way the war did not seem to change people, on the whole. During the belated celebrations for peace in 1919, she could see only a divided society, with reformers on the one hand and artists on the other, while lost in their peacetime no-man's-land drifted the wounded. She recorded her chaotic impressions of a divided society this way: "Peace Day ... the only honest people are the artists ... these social reformers & philanthropists get so out of hand, & harbor so many discreditable desires under the disguise of loving their kind ... what herd animals we are after all. ... It was a melancholy thing to see the incurable soldiers."[5]

What was remarkable about the Great War of 1914–18 was that while it should have changed so much, it had left a legacy of disillusionment, resentment, and mental and physical illness. It seemed that English people were resolutely avoiding that jolting change of perspective which Woolf was already looking forward to in her art. The war had come for many people in Europe as a welcome release from an industrial revolution that seemed to be working against them. To serve in the fields of France was a chance to escape the alienation of the city and capitalist society, to rediscover comradeship and the satisfaction of physical labor and risk. Ironically, the soldiers found themselves in the first industrialized war. Brutal economies of scale and value systems such as the "war of attrition" of General Haig totally denied individuality. As one historian says,

> It became abundantly clear in the four years of war that, in going to war, the soldier had not escaped the contradictions of capitalist society. At the front, and even at home, many realized that the war epitomized the contradiction of an "individualistic, profit-directed economy" subsisting in the midst of the "unconditional solidarity of the people." Capitalist society had not ceased being capitalist society by virtue of the war, in spite of the initial, overpowering sense of community. ...
>
> The voyage of the soldier beyond the boundaries of his home was a voyage to the place where the contradictions of industrial, capitalist society were most densely impacted. It was a voyage to the place where inequalities of wealth and status became inequalities of sacrifice and suffering.[6]

Long periods of inaction, an elusive enemy, and atrocious conditions fueled the soldiers' hatred for staff officers and those running the war. In postwar England, even though the bosses were all too visible, those same soldiers who had been robbed of their identity to become cogs in the war machine found it difficult to translate their sense of camaraderie into political action. Their schizophrenic experience often erupted in violence. For example, in 1919 there were demonstrations and mutinies on a mass scale at military camps all over Britain.[7] These actions became known as the Khaki Riots.

Willy-nilly, the war did bring about certain social changes, particularly in the status of women. The carnage of the trenches had resulted in a preponderance of women in England; in 1921, out of a population of 42.7 million, there were almost 2 million more women than men. Women had made advances that were consolidated by the war in suffrage, job opportunities, medical services, and legal status, although compared with the situation today they were still severely disadvantaged. They had also challenged social and sexual norms. Referring to the passage in *Mrs. Dalloway* about the solitary traveler, Sandra Gilbert argues that the Great War had a revolutionary effect on ideas about male and female behavior: "Topsy turvy role reversals did bring a release of female libidinal energies, as well as a liberation of female anger, which men usually found anxiety-inducing."[8] Havelock Ellis's pioneering study *The Psychology of Sex* came out in 1920, and the following year Dr. Marie Stopes founded the first birth control clinic for working women.

Despite these social advances, England was rigidly divided according to class, with very high unemployment (18 percent in 1921) and poverty. The war seemed to have benefited only the rich; in 1921, 10 percent owned 90 percent of the wealth. Although a coalition of Liberals and Labour won the election of 1923, and in 1926 the General Strike signaled the mobilization of labor and the end of Richard Dalloway's Conservatives, the workers had yet to find a real voice in Parliament.

But we should not forget the familiarity and order that London still represented for Virginia Woolf. Deceptively covering these growing social antagonisms was the rapid materialistic advancement of the middle class. The following description gives a sense of what it was like for the growing ranks of the new middle classes living in London in 1923:

> Middle income groups found that the situation was easing and, after 1923, as prices went on falling they enjoyed a gentle rise in living standards and a new degree of modest affluence. . . .
>
> They had gas or electric fires, though not yet in the main living room, where the open coal fire still seemed essential if home was to seem like home. But the shortage of domestics was being compensated for by houses that were much easier to run. Electric light was replacing gas, and all kinds of electrical consumer goods were appearing: irons, vacuum cleaners, kettles, heaters, cookers. . . .
>
> By the end of 1923 the radio was bringing a new form of entertainment into the home. Gramophones and records were of a quality previously unknown. Outside the home the music hall was giving way to the cinema. More cars were coming onto the roads every year, and with them a new species, the owner-driver. Even more popular than the car in the early twenties was the motor-cycle with sidecar. . . . On summer evenings city workers could see aeroplanes sign-writing the words "Daily Mail" in the sky in giant letters of orange and silver. Though only a few thousand people had so far ventured on air travel . . . ten-minute trips in an aeroplane were being offered to holidaymakers off the cliffs at Brighton for five shillings a time.
>
> Many of the new delights came from America: jazz music and dances like the Charleston and the Black Bottom; ice cream sodas; the new cocktail habit . . .; the most popular films; the ubiquitous Ford car. . . .
>
> The stability of the Edwardian era had gone and with it the assured viewpoint, the confident certainties about right and wrong. In such an atmosphere the teachings of Freud began to assume a new significance.[9]

Peter Walsh observes similar changes in London after his five years' absence in India: "People looked different. Newspapers seemed different. Now, for instance, there was a man writing quite openly in one of the respectable weeklies about water-closets [lavatories]. That you couldn't have done ten years ago—written quite openly about water-closets in a respectable weekly. And then this taking out a stick of rouge, or a powder-puff, and making up in public. On board ship coming home there were lots of young men and girls . . . carrying on quite openly" (80).

By the age of forty, then, Woolf had lived in three distinct social milieus: Victorian England, the liberated atmosphere of Bloomsbury, and the social turmoil following the war. The London that she writes about in *Mrs. Dalloway* is the London she experienced as a married, childless, middle-aged woman with three novels, some short stories, and many book reviews behind her. Her experience as a woman was soon to result in those theoretical classics of the feminist movement *A Room of One's Own* (1928) and *Three Guineas* (1938), but in 1925 she was already well positioned to write from a woman's perspective about the artistic, social, and political problems of the modern world. While composing *Mrs. Dalloway* she faced the same question again and again in different forms: how to imaginatively apprehend the oppositions and contradictions she saw in the people and institutions around her—the universal along with the particular? the fate of Britain along with the fate of the private soldier? public history along with private experience? the heat of the sun along with the flickering moment? physical violence along with emotional tenderness? power along with powerlessness?

It was clear to her that in order to encompass her vision, the form of fiction would have to change. As she wrote in March 1917, "The vast events now shaping across the Channel are towering over us too closely and painfully to be worked into fiction without a painful jolt in the perspective."[10] At the time of composing *Mrs. Dalloway* Woolf was turning away from successful novelists like Galsworthy and Bennett and toward the new experimental writers—Proust, Joyce, Eliot, Mansfield. All four had things to teach her.

From Proust, whose work she was reading in 1922, she learned the tunneling technique, whereby a present moment or detail could open up vistas into the past. (Jean Guiguet feels that *Mrs. Dalloway* is "the most Proustian point in Woolf's career,"[11] although it may be a coincidence of interest rather than an influence.)

From Joyce's short story "The Dead" (in *Dubliners*) she may have borrowed several ideas. Joyce's short story opens with a maid called Lily, while *Mrs. Dalloway,* which also centers on a party, opens with Clarissa talking to a maid called Lucy. In Joyce's story the memory of a dead young man, Michael Furey, intrudes into the heroine's consciousness during the party and continues to torment her when she returns to her hotel room, while in Woolf's book the intruder is another young man, Septimus. It is as if Clarissa feels the anguish of both Gretta and Gabriel in two phases: the morning visit from Peter Walsh reminds her of her own lost love, then the death of Septimus provides a kind of answer, but one that is as ambiguous as the famous closing of "The Dead."

From Joyce's novel *Ulysses,* which Woolf was also reading in 1922, she got the idea of a city novel organized around the principle of the chiming hours. As Margaret Church observes, Joyce's novel has a "Dance of the Hours" and makes reference to Big Ben. Joyce's Dublin day (also in June) is patterned on repetition and fragmentation, with public events in the street interweaving with private memories and desires just as in *Mrs. Dalloway:* "Moments of vision, of epiphany, of explosion, of breakup, of *ricorso*; the flash of light or the boom of sound, the striking of Big Ben—all represent the attempt to make something permanent of the moment, to arrest the mysterious and continual flux seen in the ambience of the great city."[12]

Woolf may have gained confidence in the idea of writing poetic prose about the modern city from the poet T. S. Eliot, a close friend. Woolf follows Eliot's critique of London society by portraying the gap between the beggars in the street and those taking tea in parlors. In his edgy conversation with Clarissa, full of subtext and lost opportunity, Peter Walsh reminds us of J. Alfred Prufrock or of the speaker in "Portrait of a Lady" (Eliot's poems of 1917). Peter may well wonder "why we have not developed into friends," while Clarissa may say, "I shall sit here, serving tea to friends." Eliot's "Rhapsody on a Windy Night" is patterned on the chiming clock and ends with "the last twist of the knife"; Peter fidgets with his pocketknife. Clocks appear in *The Waste Land* ("To where St. Mary Woolnoth kept the hours"), while Septimus, with his memories of war-torn Europe, is perhaps an example of Eliot's drowned sailor.

A fourth major influence on Woolf was the New Zealand short story writer Katherine Mansfield, whom Woolf knew and envied. In Mansfield's short story "The Garden Party" (1922) a young heroine is followed for the duration of one day as she prepares for the party, enjoys it, and then confronts the death of a man from the laboring class. Laura cannot express her conflicting emotions at the end of that story, and perhaps for all Clarissa's excitement during her own epiphany in the little room, Woolf intends us to feel that not all is resolved in her life, either. For both Laura and Clarissa, the neighbors pose challenges to their upper-class way of life.

From short stories like "The Garden Party" and "The Dead" and from the example of Proust, Woolf may have learned how to structure a longer prose work out of episodes, not divided into chapters but integrated through patterns of imagery. From Joyce and Eliot she learned that the modern city could be the setting and almost a major character in a psychological drama. But she was already aware of the powers and perils of a modern industrialized empire, because she was living at the intellectual and cultural center of London, one of the great cities of the world.

2

The Importance of the Work

In 1988 Malcolm Bradbury wrote that Woolf's importance in modern literature was beyond dispute:

> The prodigious scale and achievement of all her writing—not just the nine novels, the feminist essays, the critical books, and the biography of Roger Fry, but also the periodical articles, the diaries, and the letters, a good part of these published posthumously, and some of them still appearing—have made her work, once accused of narrowness, seem more and more central to her own time, her intellectual world, and modern artistic ideas. A second questioning of realism, a new experimentalism, and the rise of feminism have all contributed important new understandings of her work and the nature of her significance for the present.[1]

Mrs. Dalloway shows clearly, for the first time in Woolf's work, this questioning of realism (in the mind of Septimus), this experimentalism (in the book's structure), and this sophisticated feminism.

In the early 1920s Woolf was still feeling her way as a writer, despite the three novels behind her. In her first two novels, *The Voyage Out* and *Night and Day,* she had explored female consciousness in a deflected, half-understood way, packaging her exploration in the un-gainly form of the Victorian novel. With *Jacob's Room* she moved closer to creating a new form of novel and at the same time directly critiqued the English society of the Great War. What Woolf discovered in *Mrs. Dalloway* was her voice, together with her theme of human relations. Gone is the Victorian posing of her first two novels, as well as the disordered spontaneity of *Jacob's Room*. None of her subse-quent novels—*To the Lighthouse, Orlando, The Waves, The Years, Between the Acts*—moves far away from the subjects of *Mrs. Dallo-way:* war, peace, London, England, young men dying, the passing of time, the fragile web of friends and society, the place of women, and the shaping power of vision. Her "tunneling" process, combined with her seamless, imagistic prose, allowed her to explore the surfaces and depths of consciousness, while her focus on certain individuals—married couples, single men and women—allowed her to critique her society in the terms that seemed most significant to her: the relation-ship between the sexes.

This focus on the personal and the everyday was, as Woolf saw it, a new development for the English novel. In *A Room of One's Own* Woolf attacked the conventional notion of what is important to write about: "This is an important book, the critic assumes, because it deals with war. This is an insignificant book because it deals with the feel-ings of women in a drawing-room. A scene in a battlefield is more important than a scene in a shop—everywhere and much more subtly the difference of value persists."[2] So Woolf deliberately chose as hero-ine someone thoroughly domesticated and even antipathetic to her own cultural background. Through Clarissa, she explores the tension between the public woman who has surrendered her name to the convenient social fiction "Mrs. Dalloway" and the private woman preoccupied with the past, the future, and the sensuousness of the present. Through Clarissa she also shows a society in public crisis and argues that the root cause of social and political injustice is the separa-tion of "male" and "female" qualities in daily life. She takes the "big" issues and links them to "small," or domestic, answers, making causal connections between the political system and the personal predica-ments of Clarissa and Septimus.

Although many readers associate Woolf with the exploration of fine subjective emotions, we shall see that the novel has important things to say about insanity, psychiatry, politics, the monarchy, war, suicide, and homosexuality, as well as about what it feels like to sit in a park in London on a spring day. *Mrs. Dalloway* does deal with the big issues and shows that a stream-of-consciousness novel need not be a trivial affair of upper-class sensibilities. If, however, one is looking for "big answers" to what was wrong with England in the postwar years, one will be frustrated by *Mrs. Dalloway,* which seems, especially in its ending, to resist symbolism. There are not even any artists in *Mrs. Dalloway* to discuss how we might see things as they are, and see them whole. In her next novel, *To the Lighthouse,* Woolf supplied an artist figure who could work through her problems to a unifying apprehension of the opposites of male and female. When Lily Briscoe finally understands Mrs. Ramsay and summons back the memory of her— "There she sat"—the moment is of far greater aesthetic significance than Peter's moment in the last line of *Mrs. Dalloway,* because Lily has sorted out her feminist values and the novel's shape has been completed. *Mrs. Dalloway* ends with no such resolution of inner and outer worlds. All the characters have their moments of unifying vision, the climax being Clarissa's during her party, but in all these moments the aesthetic, or shape-making, sense is cut off from the business of functioning in a party or social situation.

Language and art cannot bridge this gap; they are feeble patterning devices whose systems constantly dissolve in *Mrs. Dalloway.* The people of London strain to interpret the letters made by a sign-writing plane; the trivial word spelled out is "toffee" but some observers see other letters and words, while Septimus thinks the message is especially for him. The narrator tells us that the airplane symbolizes the united prayers of human beings, "curving up and up, straight up, like something mounting in ecstasy" (33) above St. Paul's Cathedral—but the airplane's upward motion also alludes to a private moment of sexual ecstasy felt by Clarissa when she was with her friend Sally at Bourton many years earlier. In a similar confusion of private and public, the ecstatic "mounting" done by the solitary traveler is echoed in the public world by the vampirelike mounting of the goddess Conversion, by means of which the narrator sarcastically describes what passes for psychiatric treatment. While London swelters, Clarissa takes comfort in a fragment of Shakespeare: "Fear no more." Is there any "toffee" that will glue together individual needs and desires with public rituals, asks Woolf, without "converting" them to sameness? Is there a shared impulse to something greater than self that does not destroy self?

Woolf's resistance to system leads to a strong sense of openness and chance in the novel. We can contrast the open texture of *Mrs. Dalloway* with that other great novel of the modern metropolis, Joyce's *Ulysses* (1922). Joyce uses mythological and linguistic structures to pattern Leopold Bloom's day, and there are certainly image patterns in Woolf. Harvena Richter has pointed out that the day of the novel is 13 June (while Bloomsday is 16 June) and finds Joycean significance in the fact that the day is a Wednesday (from "Wodan," the god of war), that it is near the summer solstice, and that Clarissa's star sign is (perhaps) Gemini.[3] But the overwhelming sense in reading *Mrs. Dalloway* is of specificity rather than symbolism, and of the differences between characters. These obvious differences work against image patterns that are sometimes applied to two or three characters and often percolate through the text. While these patterns arise out of the surface of the London day, they remain only surface correspondences, ubiquitous but insignificant, and the whole—despite the bells tolling the hours—does not cohere.

By exploring the ability of language both to bind and to separate society, Woolf was building on *Jacob's Room* and looking ahead to experimentations with form in her later novels. *Mrs. Dalloway* is therefore important in Woolf's career as well as in the history of the novel, since it shows how traditional male-centered realism can be adapted to a female urban and political sensibility. This sensibility constantly casts an ironic gaze over the patterns and solutions that both text and reader desire and leaves us instead with problems and challenges.

3

Critical Reception

Mrs. *Dalloway* was the first of Woolf's novels to be published simultaneously in Britain and the United States. It was also the first of her
novels to be translated into French, in 1929. Some of the important
early reviews, then, came from beyond England.

Richard Hughes, a British novelist writing for the New York *Satur-
day Review of Literature,* felt that in *Mrs. Dalloway* Woolf had made
readers experience the city of London for the first time, as a crystal
rather than as a fog: "To Mrs. Woolf London exists, and to Mrs.
Woolf's readers anywhere and at any time London will exist with a
reality it can never have for those who merely live there."[1] He also
drew an insightful analogy between her "processional form" and the
paintings of Cézanne. Another American reviewer, E. W. Hawkins, felt
that Woolf was concentrating on society rather than the individual,
and he neatly reversed metaphors of perspective: "This novel throws
light, as by a prism, not upon a score of lives, but upon life as felt by a
score of people; its pursuit of Clarissa Dalloway through one day in
London leaves an impression of a real woman, but a stronger impression of a woven fabric of life, gay and tragic and dipped in mystery"
(188).

Meanwhile in England, P. C. Kennedy found fault with the novel for exactly the same reasons: it was an intellectual and finely ordered book, he felt, but "there are no people" (166). Another English reviewer felt that beyond the brilliant surface impressions, Woolf's conception of character was childish and "sentimental" (170). Arnold Bennett completed the English attack on his arch-rival by objecting that he couldn't actually finish the novel because of the absence of logical construction, the kind of thing he was able to see in "the new school of painting" (190). (Ironically, this "new school" was the post-impressionists.)

Clearly, reviewers on both sides of the Atlantic were in need of new metaphors to describe the reading process required by this modern text, and they were uneasy about the relationship in the novel between impressions and characterization, the moment and the plot. It was as much as they could do to grasp the innovative stream-of-consciousness technique without having to be sensitive as well to larger shapes, such as ironic juxtapositions and rhythms.

A more sophisticated response came from two eminent English critics. E. M. Forster, Woolf's friend of many years, took the occasion of publication to write a survey of her work for the *New Criterion*. Like Hughes, he emphasized her visual qualities ("How beautifully she sees!" [175]) and also considered her painterly sense of form, but he insisted as well that once one had "made the outline one must rub it out at once. For emphasis is fatal to the understanding of this author's work" (175). He sympathized with her attempt to create a reading experience quite different from the "gallery browsing" of the great tradition of English fiction, wherein the reading process was a familiar stroll past various framed works of art. He felt that Woolf wanted to replace the gallery with something else—perhaps, in *Mrs. Dalloway*, "a cathedral" (178). Forster remained doubtful, however, about Woolf's ability to create what he called "rounded," or fully living, characters.

In contrast, Edwin Muir appreciated her art as a valid way to evoke believable characters. He showed his understanding of Woolf's own ambitions when he praised the way her new prose technique takes the reader indirectly to psychological truths that the "psychological, analytical method" (183) could not catch. The "tunneling" method was for Muir a matter of nuance, repetition, and rhythm, whereby setting and character merge into a delicate minuet: "The characters in *Mrs. Dalloway* are real; they have their drama; but the day and the properties of the day move with them, have their dramas too; and we do not know which is the more real where all is real—whether the characters are bathed in the emanations of the day, or the day colored by the minds of the characters. The result is less akin to anything else attempted in the novel than to certain kinds of poetry, to poetry such as Wordsworth's, which records not so much a general judgment on life as a moment of serene illumination, a state of soul" (184).

An interesting early reaction was T. S. Eliot's. In 1927 he found Woolf similar to Conrad in the way she analyzed the civilized structure of things, but he also suggested that she "left out" the "deeper psychology" (192). His comments seem to refer not to *Mrs. Dalloway* but to Woolf's earlier novels and stories, because what he asks for— something "deeper" in her constructions—is surely what is supplied by the Septimus plot in *Mrs. Dalloway* and indeed by the whole process of Woolf's characters tunneling into the past.

Apart from these admiring notices, Woolf's work was generally mistaken and maligned from the thirties to the fifties. In 1931 the English critic William Empson analyzed a typical Woolfian paragraph, burlesquing her style of inconsequential complication:

We arrive, for instance, with some phrase like "and indeed" into a new sentence and a new specious present. Long, irrelevant, delicious clauses recollect the ramifications of the situation (this part corresponds to the blurring of consciousness while the heroine waits a moment to know her own mind; and it is here, by the way, that one is told most of the story); then by a twist of thought some vivid but distant detail, which she is actually conscious of, and might have been expected to finish the sentence, turns her mind towards the surface. From then on the clauses become shorter; we move towards action by a series of leaps, each, perhaps, showing what she would have done about something quite different, and just at the end, without effort, washed up by the last wave of this disturbance, like an obvious bit of grammar put in to round off the sentence, with a partly self-conscious, wholly charming humility in the heroine (how odd that the result of all this should be something so flat and domestic), we get the small useful thing she actually did do. (305)

Empson is clearly impatient with all this psychologizing; he wants more plot. He feels that the end of the novel is only a temporary pause, and he wants to be told about the meeting of Clarissa and Peter later that night (306–7).

Female critics were not necessarily more sympathetic. In 1932 Muriel Bradbrook dismissed Woolf for hiding her intellect behind "a smoke screen of feminine charm" (313). But Maud Bodkin's *Archetypal Patterns in Poetry* (1934) was the first book to concentrate on the imagery in the novel, tying it sensitively to the key element of rhythm, or rather to "the alternations of vital rhythm—a backward, inward turning of libido following the outward flow—such as Jung describes as repeating itself unconsciously in our lives 'almost continually.' So, for minutes, for an hour or two perhaps, the tide of life sets backward and each object on which [Clarissa's] eyes fall is caught into the ebb. . . . But, as she muses and her day wears on, the tide of sensibility turns again. Calm descends on her" (325). Bodkin praises Woolf's novel in feminist terms for the way it "portrays the recurring, amid the flux of an individual sensibility, of symbols of a group tradition—a tradition here mediated by no institutional or dogmatic religion, no profound literary study, only by lines from casual reading that have become means of reference to ideals suffused through personal relationship." Here, however, as with other critics sensitive to Woolf's artistry, there is a desire for homogeneity and unity. For Bodkin there should be no deep, unresolvable tension between the inward and outward flows, between the ideals and the personal relationships.

The chapters on the novel that appeared in the standard early studies of Woolf's work (by Bennett, Guiguet, Chambers, and others) tended to emphasize Woolf's achievement of a sensitive style, as well as the triumph of Clarissa at the end of the novel. A more recent example of this kind of approach is offered by Howard Harper, who focuses on "the essential dialectical struggle . . . between the opposite adaptations to the world which are represented by Clarissa and by Septimus."[2] While Harper recognizes that the "narrative consciousness" is to some degree alienated from Clarissa's world, he eventually sides with Clarissa because, while Septimus has just as much sensitivity, he has "none of her empathy." A. D. Moody's 1963 study, *Virginia Woolf,* is a rare dissenting voice in that it recognizes a causal connection between Clarissa's world and Septimus's plight. She calls *Mrs. Dalloway* "a minor and imperfect novel" largely because while it sets out to condemn Clarissa for her "glittering triviality," it fails fully to confront Clarissa with Septimus's persecution. Thus "the very grave criticism of a society that kills the soul comes with very little weight or force."[3]

More recent criticism may be roughly divided into three kinds: stylistic, sociopsychological, and feminist. A good example of stylistic criticism is Hermione Lee's *The Novels of Virginia Woolf.* Lee begins with the unit of the sentence and shows how Woolf wanted to extend its range and suppleness, to create "a form patterned like waves on a pond rather than a railway line."[4] She then considers the larger units, showing how we are given various facets of Clarissa's character as she is seen by other characters, and finally as she is seen in time, or what Lee calls a "consciousness time" that opens up vistas to significant past moments. Allen McLaurin extends this stylistic analysis to suggest that through her "keyboard" of symbols and images Woolf critiques our separation of images from reality.[5] For Maria DiBattista, the book is "a healthy work of the imagination" because in it Woolf considers and rejects the archetypes and mythos (such as the descent into Hades) offered to her by the male imagination, in society and in literature.[6] DiBattista, like J. Hillis Miller, emphasizes the qualities of the narrating presence in the novel, a presence that transcends the difficulties of the characters and offers various solutions to their problems. For Miller, "narration is repetition as the raising of the dead."[7] He argues that the day in *Mrs. Dalloway* is "a general day of recollection" for all the characters and that the narrative voice speaks for a "universal, impersonal mind" that unites the characters at a deep level.[8] Eventually, he says, the book itself, as an artifact, triumphs over death in a way that no life, including Woolf's own, could ever do. (The work of other stylistic critics, such as Daiches and Humphrey, is discussed in chapter 5.)

The second critical approach stresses the sociopsychological context. Zwerdling's "*Mrs. Dalloway* and the Social System" regards the novel as a presentation and critique of the state of England in 1923, while Leaska's *The Novels of Virginia Woolf* emphasizes the failed marriages of both Clarissa and Septimus and the repressive notions of homosexual love held by society at the time. Beker argues that "the city defines the characters," and Meisel agrees that "the figure of the map and the territory it represents and organizes is a particularly resonant one given the way the novel's interest in political economy and imperialism underlies all the metaphors of exchange, psychical and commercial alike, of which life in *Mrs. Dalloway* is composed."[9] Susan Squier takes this idea much further in her study *Virginia Woolf and London* (1985). For her, the social world of London is male dominated, and Clarissa can survive there only by becoming a kind of background for her menfolk; she is the "classic female product of a patriarchal culture".[10] Squier shows how the various perambulations of the main characters explore the public/private dichotomy of living in a city. For example, London society, sexually polarized and technological as it is, mirrors as well as causes Septimus's suffering. Eventually Septimus's death is used by Clarissa as a sentimental focus for all that is wrong with the city, so that she can continue with her "sinister" enjoyment of it.[11]

Critics like Trombley, Rose, and Spilka place the novel in the context of Woolf's own life, stressing the themes of either Woolf's insanity or her grieving for her dead mother. Less personally, Harold Bloom, editing a recent anthology of criticism on *Mrs. Dalloway*, concludes his introduction by stating, "It seems . . . difficult to defend *Mrs. Dalloway* from moral judgments that call Woolf's stance wholly nihilistic."[12]

The third critical approach to the novel combines elements of the first two with feminist concerns, and constitutes the most astute and exciting of recent studies. Many of these consider Clarissa to be a victim of society or, more extremely, a frustrated lesbian (judging by her behavior with Sally Seton and subsequent celibacy). For Ellen Rosenman, Clarissa secures her symbolic role of femininity and motherhood only at great cost, by evading such central female experiences as sexual pleasure and friendship with one's own sex; eventually she "transforms herself into an artifact"[13] for the sake of male society at large.

Others find a more positive aspect to Woolf's style and themes. For Elizabeth Abel, the novel rewrites and revises the incidents of a Jane Austen novel thirty years on, with the romantic themes still unresolved: "Woolf structures Clarissa's development as a stark binary opposition between past and present, nature and culture, feminine and masculine dispensations. . . . Versions of this opposition reverberate throughout the novel in rhetorical and narrative juxtapositions. The developmental plot, which slides beneath the more familiar romantic plot through the gap between Peter's and Clarissa's memories, exists as two contrasting moments and the silence adjoining and dividing them."[14] For Abel, while the sacrifices made to the system by wives like Richard's Clarissa and Septimus's Rezia are made clear by Woolf, Clarissa does learn through Septimus's death to work through her past and accept growth into the future.

Despite its forbidding density, Minow-Pinkney's recent feminist study brings together the best insights of recent deconstructionist criticism to move usefully between content and form. Like many recent stylistic critics, she focuses on the narrator and argues that Woolf was concerned to show how one may deny the "transcendental unified subject" identified with the male patriarchy, not only through the way Clarissa acts but also, and more importantly, through the way the narrator controls the novel. The narrator traces a delicate path between the marginalizations of silence and madness, just as Clarissa does.

There has been one book-length study of the novel, by Jeremy Hawthorn. He sees *Mrs. Dalloway* as an examination of "the social phenomenon which we call alienation."[15] The split between public and private worlds that Squier attributes to a patriarchal society is a division that Hawthorn attributes to modern capitalist society—perhaps they amount to the same thing. Hawthorn sees Septimus's madness as an extreme form of alienation, and he contrasts Septimus's gift of death with Clarissa's gift of her party, which we are meant to see "seriously" as "a symbol of that feminine gift for bringing people together."[16] Hawthorn concludes that Woolf's solution is inadequate because "Virginia Woolf herself lacks the sort of experience and knowledge which would allow her to present solutions to Clarissa's problems more convincing and lasting than that of the party."[17]

Perhaps the low point of Woolf criticism came in 1955 when Lord Snow, the novelist and essayist, attacked her for having "no roots in society."[18] All three approaches to *Mrs. Dalloway* that are described above—the stylistic, the sociopsychological, and the feminist—amply demonstrate that this novel, perhaps more than any other of Woolf's novels, squarely addresses the central issues of society then and now: the relationships between self and society, male and female, war and peace, and the price of civility.

4

Composition

Having traced the artistic evolution of the novel, we should now consider its "psychological" evolution as a response to Woolf's own struggle with mental illness. When Woolf wrote, in the introduction to the American Modern Library edition of *Mrs. Dalloway,* that "books are the flowers or fruit stuck here and there on a tree which has its roots deep down in the earth of our earliest life, of our first experiences," she intimated that her novel does indeed reach down into the deepest experiences of its creator, in particular into the recesses of her own subconscious—those aspects of her mental life which Woolf encountered all too frequently during her periodic bouts of mental illness.

From the time of her mother's death in 1895 when Woolf was thirteen, the novelist was often mentally ill, most seriously in 1904, 1913, 1915, and 1941. She took great interest in the personalities of her successive physicians. The names of the psychologists with whom Woolf came into contact and the names associated with her periods of illness haunt *Mrs. Dalloway:* in 1897 Woolf wrote of a "Dr. Seton" (suggesting Sally Seton); in 1922 one of her doctors, Maurice Craig, delivered the Bradshaw lecture to the Royal College of Physicians (suggesting Dr. Bradshaw); and to complete this linguistic nexus, the name of the physician most involved with Woolf was Dr. Henry Head (which is where Woolf's novel takes place, in the heads of her characters). The Stephen family physician was Dr. George Savage, whose attitude toward mental illness was quite advanced for his time (he was born in 1842), although Woolf later felt that he was tyrannical and true to his name. He advocated rest, walks, and nourishment for his patients, and in 1884 (the year he published his *Insanity and Allied Neuroses,* revised in 1907), he declared himself against the constant observation of suicidal patients in mental homes; he felt that a certain risk was necessary if one was to encourage such patients to live normal lives.[1] But Savage also discouraged education for women, on the grounds that it would make them unfit for domestic work. In 1912 he counseled the Woolfs not to have children, because of Virginia's condition.

Many doctors had a far more brutal attitude toward mental illness. Stephen Trombley has shown that among the physicians who treated Woolf—Dr. Maurice Wright, Dr. D. J. Fergusson, Sir George Savage, Dr. Henry Head, Dr. T. B. Hyslop, and Dr. Maurice Craig— were several whose views were authoritarian and crude. For example, "[Dr. Craig's] primary method of treating Virginia in the years following her suicide attempt was to get her to eat as much as possible."[2] (In the novel, Dr. Bradshaw's regimen, observes the narrator, would result in a man who went in weighing seven stone six coming out weighing twelve [110].) Dr. Hyslop said that the works shown at the 1910 postimpressionist exhibition were painted by mentally unstable people and, in *The Borderland* (1924), argued that doctors had a duty to halt the degeneration of humanity. One of Woolf's biographers concludes that "the hopeless meddling of consultants . . . is distilled in her fictional portrait of a Harley Street nerve specialist, Sir William Bradshaw."[3]

Woolf took a keen interest in the growth of the science of psychology in general. In 1910 she wrote that Miss Thomas, who ran the Burley mental home where Woolf stayed on four occasions from 1910 to 1915, confirmed her own theory about the cathartic, health-giving effect of emotional stimulation: "Miss Thomas says that these excitements are the wine of life. This bears out my theory, based on Aunt Fisher, and all the other sepulchral women, that what people like is feeling—it don't matter what."[4] In the novel, part of Septimus's tragedy is that he is persecuted not for *what* he feels but because he feels at all; his London is a society of people determined not to feel. Woolf observed that even people who advocate the health of "strong" feeling often have a dictatorial conviction about which feelings are appropriate. This point is illustrated by Woolf's own relationship with Jean Thomas, which was particularly close but deteriorated over the years as Woolf sensed Thomas's authoritarianism and insistence on religion. (Stephen Trombley follows this relationship and suggests that Jean Thomas was the model for Miss Kilman.[5] She could equally be a prototype for Bradshaw.)

Woolf's notion of the importance to mental health of uncensored feeling, particularly for women, strengthened over the years. By 1924 she was writing to Jacques Raverat (a French painter Woolf had met when he was at Cambridge) that her own illness had a positive value. The Stephen family tradition of "taste" and incessant criticism was in her view tempered by her bouts of irrationality and by her subsequent understanding of the place of emotions and the irrational in people's lives: "My madness has saved me," she said.[6] It is difficult for us now to appreciate the stress of living the life of a Victorian gentlewoman: instead of a constant, natural letting off of steam through spontaneous acts, there were repression, ignorance, and lack of privacy, all of which contributed to the kinds of violent swings from normalcy to madness that Woolf experienced.

Woolf's account of how the original Clarissa "split" into the party hostess and the self that kills itself (Septimus) has encouraged us to see the novel as an allegory of one person's spiritual state: a psychological enactment or psychodrama. But by transferring Clarissa's own suicidal impulses to another quite separate character, Woolf also strengthened her political critique by connecting the private world, with its dimension of time, to the public world, with its dimension of space. Clarissa's repressions are linked to those which maintain the power structure of London society, a sophisticated force that now reaches outward in space, across London, to ensnare another citizen as in a web. While *Mrs. Dalloway* has an intimate connection with Woolf's own history of mental suffering, this strategy enabled Woolf to articulate her view that mental illness is very much a social construct with social causes. By following the compositional process we can see how Woolf's interest in the mind and in society gradually merged into this inseparable complex.

During and after the "Great" War, Woolf and her friends were preoccupied with the idea of civilization and with trying to define what values their own inherited Victorian civilization stood for. In 1916 Woolf's friend Lytton Strachey offered to the British public his famous defense for his pacifist stand, a defense that was only slightly in jest: "I am the civilization they are fighting to defend." Strachey went on to write *Eminent Victorians* (1919), an extremely important book in twentieth-century English social history. It was the first book to be iconoclastic about the Victorian age, its civilization, and its heroes: Cardinal Manning, General Gordon, Arnold of Rugby School, and Florence Nightingale. It was also one of the first works in English to be informed by the new psychoanalytic notions of repression and the subconscious (Strachey's brother James was the translator of Freud's works into English, and the Hogarth Press was his publisher). *Eminent Victorians* is sly and sarcastic, its tone reinforcing the idea of its preface that there was dirty linen from the Victorian cupboard to be aired but that the exposing must be done with delicacy. By using metaphors of surface and depth and by wickedly co-opting the strategies of the military, Strachey suggested that there was a split between the outward show of a civilization and the private desires and fears of its citizens. His method in *Eminent Victorians* parodied this state of affairs since it presented an apparently untroubled, approving surface. In his preface, however, Strachey explains how the biographer "will attack his subject in unexpected places; he will fall upon the flank, or the rear; he will shoot a sudden, revealing searchlight into obscure recesses, hitherto undivined. He will row out over that great ocean of material, and lower down into it, here and there, a little bucket, which will bring up to the light of day some characteristic specimen, from those far depths, to be examined with a careful curiosity."[7]

Woolf also reappraised the Victorians and introduced these psychological ideas in her first novel, *The Voyage Out* (1915), which studies, albeit in a feverish and half-formed way, feminism and psychosis. *Night and Day* (1919) continued her inner exploration, but in July 1919 her novelistic attention turned to the larger public world around her. Woolf wrote in her diary, "The effect of the war would be worth describing."[8] *Jacob's Room* (1922) was a partial answer to this desire, focusing as it does on a typical young Englishman who disappears into the mud of Flanders. But what comes to fascinate Woolf in that novel is the very act of apprehension, the novelist's attempt to imagine a character. The author's questionings break apart the traditional form of fiction as she attempts to locate the psychological reality of her hero, young Jacob Flanders. The narrator hovers over Jacob's room in the same way that we try to get to know someone in real life. He remains elusive for two reasons—he has been reared to obey and he has been reared to be an English gentleman ("He has been taught at his public school that feeling is bad form," as E. M. Forster puts it in an essay)[9]—and what inner life he may have is difficult to convey, since conventional methods of characterization do not correspond to life as we feel it. In this novel, then, Woolf criticizes both the civilized society and the civilized art of her time. She addresses the problem of trying to evoke a whole society in fiction, especially one as disparate and divided as English postwar society. She laments the necessity of choosing among the various classes and occupations of people in London: "But no—we must choose."[10] For much of the novel, the narrator is preoccupied with classes of people and dimensions of experience that a conventional narrative might miss. For example, Julia Eliot, prototype of Mrs. Dalloway, checks her watch on her way to Bruton Street, but "there rose in her mind a curious sadness, as if time and eternity showed through skirts and waistcoats, and she saw people passing tragically to destruction" (168). If one moves off the beaten path in the city of London, Woolf suggests, one might find strangeness and violence: "As frequent as street corners in Holborn are these chasms in the continuity of our ways. Yet we keep straight on" (95). London becomes a metaphor for the human mind, and the life going on inside buildings and up dark alleys eludes the traditional narrator trained to focus on "civilized" values and themes. Likewise, the threat of disruption or the possibility of other lives and sensations remains beyond the imagination of most of the characters in *Jacob's Room*. Only Mrs. Flanders hears the guns in France that rumble ominously, "as if nocturnal women were beating great carpets" (175).

Near the end of *Jacob's Room*, Woolf turns from these metaphorical problems of technique to a direct, trenchant critique of British imperialism. On the one hand are the politicians, "manfully determined . . . to control the course of events. . . . [A]ltogether they looked too red, fat, pale, lean, to be dealing, as the marble heads had dealt, with the course of history" (172). On the other hand are the common sailors and soldiers, like Jacob, dying in quiet, patriotic obedience: "Like blocks of tin soldiers the army covers the corn-field, moves up the hillside, stops, reels slightly this way and that, and falls flat, save that, through field-glasses, it can be seen that one or two pieces still agitate up and down like fragments of broken match-stick" (155). Woolf gives us a distinct perspective here in order to shock us into sympathy and to make us realize how easily we slip into habits of abstraction. Her scorn for the politicians and theoreticians who play with people's lives erupts into a sarcastic attack on diplomacy in the last pages of the novel: "These actions . . . are the strokes which oar the world forward, they say. . . . It is thus that we live, they say, driven by an unseizable force. They say that the novelists never catch it" (155).

For Woolf, political and aesthetic revolution had begun to seem identical. Against the public tragedy wrought by "them" who have no time for individuals or for art, Woolf the artist opposes the ordinariness of such domestic details as sunlight striking shaving-glasses, which compose "the bright, inquisitive, armored, resplendent, summer's day, which has long since vanquished chaos; which has dried the melancholy mediaeval mists; drained the swamp and stood glass and stone upon it; and equipped our brains and bodies with such an armory of weapons that merely to see the flash and thrust of limbs engaged in the conduct of daily life is better than the old pageant of armies drawn out in battle array upon the plain" (165). Merely to apprehend daily life, to value it and make it into art, is therefore a subversive political act that simultaneously attacks "civilized" art, "civilized" psychology, and "civilized" values. In the postwar years this "home front" battle of perspective—redefining what is valuable—preoccupied Woolf, but it was not until April 1922 that she wrote to T. S. Eliot that she was finishing her short story "Mrs. Dalloway in Bond Street"[11] (it was published in the *Dial* in July 1923), the story that opened the way to Woolf's less theoretical, more inclusive examination of postwar England.

That short story, which became the first pages of the novel, shows Clarissa's stiff upper lip and her pride, which "held her erect, inheriting, handing on, acquainted with discipline and with suffering."[12] This earlier Clarissa actually notices, on Bond Street, Lady Bexborough, that same woman who opened a bazaar while holding the telegram containing news of her son's death in France. "There she is," says Clarissa, anticipating Peter Walsh's final comments about herself, and admiring a similar quality of fortitude and elegance in Lady Bexborough. But Clarissa also senses an unease about the great woman—"They say she is sick of it all."[13] In this way those facets of Clarissa's character which we must deduce in the novel are more vividly defined in the story. She has an "extraordinarily deep instinct" to bow to men like Hugh Whitbread; she wants to read about death (although the moderns, unlike Shelley, have nothing to say on the subject); she does not believe in God, partly because she senses the total fragmentation of her society in the distance between herself and the shop woman, nor does she believe in charity to the lower classes: "Dick had shown her the folly of giving impulsively. It was much more important, he said, to get trade with China. . . . There she was in her place. So was Dick. Selling gloves was her job."[14]

Here the sentence "There she was," which concludes the novel, takes on less admirable shades of meaning, since it is used, as it was when Clarissa described Lady Bexborough, to support the class system and the status quo. This Clarissa is clearly uncertain and unhappy about her role in British society, but she gathers herself together, martyrlike, determined to play her part "for the sake of others." That shop woman, thinks Clarissa, would be much more unhappy were she *not* able to believe—in Clarissa, in the empire, in royalty, in class, in the system. The story ends with the backfire of a car outside, a car that might be carrying the prime minister. But this ominous sign reminds Clarissa neither of the war nor of the prime minister (at least if it does, she is certainly not going to acknowledge it outwardly). Instead, it provides a moment for Clarissa to demonstrate her unflappability and to close ranks with her kind by saluting the other "woman of substance" in the shop: "There was a violent explosion in the street outside. The shopwomen cowered behind the counters. But Clarissa, sitting very upright, smiled at the other lady. 'Miss Anstruther!' she exclaimed."[15]

The other short stories Woolf wrote around this time on her favorite theme of what she called the "party-consciousness" also enlarge Clarissa and her world. In "A Summing Up" the heroine, Sasha Latham, thinks of her hostess that she "had laid paving stones over the bog."[16] This reminder is common in Woolf's writings—that London had once been a wild swamp and that it is only through the strenuous efforts of civilized people over hundreds of years that the modern metropolis was created. But "A Summing Up" also points to the other side of progress, an aspect Woolf was to articulate through Septimus: the cost of repression, of pushing down the swamps of nature and maintaining that civilized surface of concrete and macadam. At the end of this story Sasha, who has gone outside to escape the noise and pressures of a party, feels (as Clarissa does) that she must return and play her part as a well-mannered young lady. As she goes, from beyond the garden wall "the usual, terrible, sexless, inarticulate voice rang out; a shriek, a cry. And the widow bird, startled, flew away . . . what she called her soul."[17] In the novel this scene survives in Clarissa's meditation on the old woman opposite, ponderings that facilitate her finding rather than losing her soul—at least, that is what Clarissa feels.

By August 1922 Woolf had begun to enlarge the story into a novel: "For my own part I am laboriously dredging my mind for Mrs. Dalloway & bringing up light buckets."[18] (This image of psychological depths she probably got from Strachey's preface to *Eminent Victorians*.) She was unsure where to go with her idea and how to include other reactions to the prime minister's car ("Shall I write the next chapter of Mrs. Dalloway—if she is to have a next chapter; & shall it be *The Prime Minister*?"). But in October an old family friend, Kitty Maxse, fainted, fell over a banister, and died (some said it was suicide),[19] following which event Woolf felt free to write objectively about her parents' generation. As she observed in 1925, "There were originals for some of the people in *Mrs. Dalloway;* but very far away—people I last saw ten years ago and even then, did not know well. Those are the people I like to write about."[20] (There may be a reason Woolf said she enjoyed writing about people from "ten years ago": ten years earlier exactly, in 1913, she had attempted suicide herself, with an overdose of veronal.)

Two days after Kitty Maxse's death, Woolf was recording: "At Home: or The Party. . . . This is to be a short book consisting of six or seven chapters each complete separately, yet there must be some sort of fusion."[21] "The Prime Minister" became chapter 2 of the novel, in which H. Z. Prentice, a middle-class radical and prototype for Septimus, is angered at the patriotic reaction of Edgar J. Watkiss to the prime minister's car. At this point, Woolf was thinking only of Clarissa as a focus. As she wrote in her introduction to the American edition of *Mrs. Dalloway* (1928), "In the first version Septimus, who later is intended to be her double, had no existence. . . . Mrs. Dalloway was originally to kill herself, or perhaps merely to die at the end of the party."

The real breakthrough—the split into two narratives—came shortly after, on 14 October: "Mrs. Dalloway has branched into a book; & I adumbrate here a study of insanity & suicide: the world seen by the sane & the insane side by side—something like that. Septimus Smith?—is that a good name?—& to be more close to the fact than *Jacob*. . . . I shall finish the *Prime Minister* in another week."[22] Woolf began to struggle with the technical challenge:

> Suppose it to be connected in this way:
> Sanity & insanity.
> Mrs. Dalloway seeing the truth, Septimus Smith seeing the insane truth. . . .

> The pace is to be given by the gradual increase of Septimus's insanity on the one side; by the approach of the party on the other. . . .
> The Question is whether the inside of the mind in both Mrs. Dalloway & Septimus Smith can be made luminous—that is to say the stuff of the book—lights on it coming from external sources.[23]

In November, Woolf introduced Rezia and indicated that her early plans for Clarissa's death had now been transferred to Septimus, who was to be real "only in so far as she sees him. Otherwise to exist in his view of things: which is always to be contrasting with Mrs. Dalloway's. . . . Suppose the idea of the book is the contrast between life & death. All inner feelings to be lit up. The two minds. Mrs. Dalloway and Septimus.. . . . All must bear finally upon the party at the end; which expresses life, in every variety & full of antic[ipa]tion; while Septimus dies."[24] The close of 1922 saw Woolf trying out various formal arrangements, such as doing away with chapters[25] and organizing the novel "like acts of a play into 5 or six scenes. . . . [Mrs. Dalloway] must be seen by other people."[26]

By March 1923 the character of Septimus was taking clearer shape: "a man of about twenty seven, with eyes rather far apart, a pale face, and very white teeth. . . . His heart was beating very fast. Everything had momentarily become very splendid and very simple. Yet physically he felt as if unless something cool and firm restrained his heart it would fly into pieces. . . . 'As I am going to die I will kill the Prime Minister.' "[27] In the final version, of course, Septimus's murderous impulses are turned in upon himself. In May 1923 came another breakthrough, with the invention of Peter Walsh,[28] who would shed another light on Clarissa and also provide a link with Septimus. June 1923 saw Woolf concerned with her message, in two diary entries:

> I want to give the slipperiness of the soul. I have been too tolerant often. The truth is people scarcely care for each other. They have this insane instinct for life. But they never become attuned to anything outside themselves.[29]

> I want to give life & death, sanity & insanity; I want to criticize the social system, & to show it at work, at its most intense. . . . I think it

most important in this book to go for the central things, even
though they don't submit, as they should however, to beautification
in language. . . . The design is so queer & so masterful. I'm always
having to wrench my substance to fit it.[30]

In August she was pondering how to catch the sequence of thoughts in
a deranged mind; she had a "sense of falling through into discoveries—
like a trap door opening. . . . There should be a fairly logical transition
in Septimus's mind."[31] Gradually the whole shape of the book was
becoming definite in her mind, as she saw how she could hang her
psychological forays from the surface events of one day. She was excited by her progress: "I should say a good deal about *The Hours,* &
my discovery; how I dig out beautiful caves behind my characters; I
think that gives exactly what I want; humanity, humor, depth. The idea
is that the caves shall connect, & each comes to daylight at the present
moment—Dinner!"[32]

Although the writing of Septimus's last hours became exhausting
to her, Woolf found relief in this new technique of tunneling. She
wrote in her diary: "I am now in the thick of the mad scene in Regent's
Park. . . . I am stuffed with ideas for it. I feel I can use up everything
I've ever thought. Certainly, I'm less coerced than I've yet been. The
doubtful point is I think the character of Mrs. Dalloway. It may be too
stiff, too glittering & tinsely—but then I can bring innumerable other
characters to her support. . . . It took me a year's groping to discover
what I call my tunnelling process, by which I tell the past by
instalments, as I have need of it."[33]

In March 1924 the Woolfs moved from Richmond to 52 Tavistock Square, Bloomsbury, in central London, where Woolf began
rewriting the novel. The move back to town made Woolf look upon
the city with fresh eyes: "Why do I love it [London] so much? . . . For
it is stony hearted, and callous. The tradespeople don't know one."[34]
But the city had the advantage of keeping her afloat in society, so that
she would not fall into mental cracks like those she was composing for
Septimus: "One of these days I will write about London, and how it
takes up the private life and carries it on, without any effort. Faces

passing lift up my mind; prevent it from settling, as it does in the stillness at Rodmell. . . . But my mind is full of *The Hours*."[35] Woolf gained confidence in her method; in May she published the theoretical essay "Mr. Bennett and Mrs. Brown" and in August was well along with revisions to the novel: "I think I can go straight at the grand party & so end; forgetting Septimus, which is very intense & ticklish business, & jumping Peter Walsh eating his dinner, which may be some obstacle too. But I like going from one lighted room to another, such is my brain to me; lighted rooms; and the walks in the field are corridors."[36] Her final comment on the novel before completing it on 9 October pointed to her desired quality of solidity and lightness in *Mrs. Dalloway:* "It is to be a most complicated spirited solid piece, knitting together everything & ending on three notes, at different stages of the staircase, each saying something to sum up Clarissa. Who shall say these things? Peter, Richard, & Sally Seton perhaps. . . . Suppose one can keep the quality of a sketch in a finished & composed work? That is my endeavor."[37]

Woolf looked back with pleasure at the speed of the composition process and felt she had exorcised the spell laid by John Middleton Murry, who, in his review of *Jacob's Room,* argued that she could not create plot.[38] All that remained was for her to revise the short story "Mrs. Dalloway in Bond Street" as the opening to the novel, and in November to revise "the mad chapters of *Mrs. Dalloway.* My wonder is whether the book would have been better without them. . . . The reviewers will say that it is disjointed because of the mad scenes not connecting with the Dalloway scenes."[39] Despite this apprehension about the novel's coherence, in December came her private seal of approval: *Mrs. Dalloway,* she wrote after reading it through, "seems to leave me plunged deep in the richest strata of my mind."[40]

A Reading

✳

5

Style

WOOLF'S THEORY OF FICTION

The first of two key statements about Woolf's theoretical position was made in 1919 in an essay entitled "Modern Fiction." Woolf was ready to take up arms against what she called the "materialists" of fiction: Wells, Bennett, and Galsworthy. Somehow in their fiction "life" escaped. What was this "life"?

> Examine for a moment an ordinary mind on an ordinary day. The mind receives a myriad impressions—trivial, fantastic, evanescent, or engraved with the sharpness of steel. From all sides they come, an incessant shower of innumerable atoms; and as they fall, as they shape themselves into the life of Monday or Tuesday, the accent falls differently from of old; the moment of importance came not here but there; so that if a writer were a free man and not a slave, if he could write what he chose, and not what he must, if he could base his work upon his own feeling and not upon convention, there would be no plot, no comedy, no tragedy, no love interest or catastrophe in the accepted style, and perhaps not a single button sewn on as the Bond Street tailors would have it. Life is not a series of gig lamps symmetrically arranged; but a luminous halo, a semi-transparent

envelope surrounding us from the beginning of consciousness to the end.[1]

As she worked on *Mrs. Dalloway* during 1923, Woolf again began using this notion of the "luminous" mind. She wanted her characters' minds to be "lit up," and the source of light was to be an external force as well as an internal stream of consciousness. Characters would reflect upon one another as well as on themselves, like lighthouses—an idea that anticipates the central image of her next novel, *To the Lighthouse*. It was a technique that would work only in a crowded city or party scene, with the friends of Clarissa or the doctors around Septimus acting as stage lights to illuminate the central figures on the stage. At the same time, Woolf preserved the privacy of the individual halo. Although Clarissa and Septimus almost meet among the Bond Street tailors, they move apart (see Figures 1b and 1c), and the connections between them remain in their own minds only. Clock chimes and signwriting planes signify the common physical space shared by the characters, but their mental space is filled with their own affairs. Even Peter, the unsuspecting go-between from one plot to another, misinterprets both Septimus and Clarissa.

As for the subject matter and plot of her new novel, Woolf discussed these in *Jacob's Room*. She would not give us the great men and great events of her time; she would focus on ordinary people during ordinary days. She insisted on this focus in the second key theoretical document, her 1924 essay "Mr. Bennett and Mrs. Brown." Here was the fruit of a decade of reviewing novels: another attack on the (mostly male) Edwardian novelists, such as Galsworthy, Bennett, and Wells. According to Woolf, "in or about December, 1910, human character changed."[2] This remark was a slightly cliquish reference to the First Post-Impressionist Exhibition organized by her friend Roger Fry, but it had a symbolic point: despite the outcry by the British establishment, that exhibition had publicly acknowledged the existence of the subconscious and the primacy of how we see (or the "impression" on the individual) over what we see. The implications of the new attitude stretched beyond aesthetics and psychology. Woolf is quite explicit in her essay that the change is social and revolutionary: "All human relations have shifted—those between masters and servants, husbands and wives, parents and children."[3]

Even the form of Woolf's speech, which she gave at Cambridge, was revolutionary, for she chose to tell a story. It concerned the novelist's fascination with a little old lady sitting opposite her in a railway carriage whom the novelist decides to call "Mrs. Brown," because, Woolf said, "I believe that all novels begin with an old lady in the corner opposite. I believe that all novels, that is to say, deal with character, and that it is to express character—not to preach doctrines, sing songs, or celebrate the glories of the British Empire, that the form of the novel, so clumsy, verbose, and undramatic, so rich, elastic, and alive, has been evolved."[4] Woolf welcomes writers like Strachey, Eliot, and Joyce (none of them much admired by the Establishment in the early twenties), who, she feels, are remaining loyal to Mrs. Brown and her psychological reality rather than to the scientific reality of railway carriages, clothes, timetables, and the weather. Her own novels, beginning with *Mrs. Dalloway,* would be "rich, elastic and alive" and would not desert Mrs. Brown, whether her avatars were a shell-shocked soldier, a society hostess, or an old lady in a window.

Woolf's theory has implications beyond aesthetics and psychology. If the nature of perception has changed, then it has changed for both the writer and the reader of novels as well as for the novel's characters. What kind of structure can a novelist use, if not a strong "external" narrative? How can the novelist avoid a series of tremulous impressions about nothing very much? The answer, for novelist as for painter, lies in patterning, or significant form. Here we reach the mystic conclusion of Woolf's idea of "life" because the artist observes and articulates the connections between individuals' experience and so asserts a transcendent unity. In her "Sketch of the Past" Woolf stated this artistic creed, using the same notions of context and connection that she used to describe her mother's personality:

Perhaps this is the strongest pleasure known to me. It is the rapture I get when in writing I seem to be discovering what belongs to what;

making a scene come right; making a character come together. From this I reach what I might call a philosophy; at any rate it is a constant idea of mine; that behind the cotton wool is hidden a pattern; that we—I mean all human beings—are connected with this; that the whole world is a work of art; that we are parts of the work of art. *Hamlet* or a Beethoven quartet is the truth about this vast mass that we call the world. But there is no Shakespeare, there is no Beethoven; certainly and emphatically there is no God; we are the words; we are the music; we are the thing itself.[5]

It is the artist's task not to judge but to show connections. How Woolf managed this task in the polarized and politically unstable world of postwar London is the subject of the remainder of this chapter.

Close Analysis of a Passage

The passage we will examine comes after Peter Walsh has visited Clarissa. He stands outside her house on Victoria Street, at 11:30 A.M., thinking what a fool he has made of himself:

As a cloud crosses the sun, silence falls on London; and falls on the mind. Effort ceases. Time flaps on the mast. There we stop; there we stand. Rigid, the skeleton of habit alone upholds the human frame. **Where there is nothing,**
5   Peter Walsh said to himself; feeling hollowed out, utterly empty within. **Clarissa refused me,** he thought. He stood there thinking, **Clarissa refused me.**
     Ah, said St Margaret's, *like* a hostess who comes into her drawing-room on the very stroke of the hour and finds her
10   guests there already. I am not late. No, it is precisely half-past eleven, she says. Yet, though she is perfectly right, her voice, being the voice of the hostess, is reluctant to inflict its individuality. Some grief for the past holds it back; some concern for the present. It is half-past eleven, she says, and
15   the sound of St Margaret's glides into the recesses of the heart and buries itself in ring after ring of sound, *like* something alive which wants to confide itself, to disperse

itself, to be, with a tremor of delight, at rest,—*like*
Clarissa herself, thought Peter Walsh, **coming down the**
20   **stairs on the stroke of the hour in white. It is**
Clarissa herself, he thought, with a deep emotion, and an
extraordinarily clear yet puzzling recollection of her, *as if*
this bell had come into the room years ago, where they sat at
some moment of great intimacy, and had gone from one to the
25   other and had left, *like* a bee with honey, laden with the
moment. **But what room? What moment? And why had**
he been so profoundly happy when the clock was
striking? Then, as the sound of St Margaret's languished, he
thought, **she has been ill,** and the sound expressed languor
30   and suffering. **It was her heart,** he remembered; and the
sudden loudness of the final stroke tolled for death that
surprised in the midst of life, Clarissa falling where she
stood, in her drawing-room. **No! No!** he cried. **She is not**
dead! I am not old, he cried, and marched up Whitehall *as*
35   *if* there rolled down to him, vigorous, unending, his future.
(55–56)

Peter's thoughts (in boldface) are direct monologue, except for the indirect monologue of "And why had he been so profoundly happy when the clock was striking?" (l.27) and "It was her heart" (l.30). The narrator uses the present tense ("crosses") and first person plural ("we") to invite the reader to stand with Peter on that London street, to feel the moment with him. By means of an extended conceit we find ourselves at a morning tea with Peter, and St. Margaret is our hostess (it still appears to be "our" heart where the chime buries itself [l. 16]). We are made to feel the pleasure and limitations of high society, its restful formality yet its lack of individuality.

The narrator supplies the two governing similes of the passage (the similes in the passage are italicized): the skeleton of London and the personification of St. Margaret's church as a hostess. In both cases, Peter "chimes in" to agree with the simile and extend it. In the first case he thinks of his own skeleton (l. 3), his being emptied of love and the past since Clarissa appears to have denied him fellowship as she denied him marriage thirty years earlier. The phrase "Time flaps on the mast" (l. 2) comes from Woolf's diary, where she equated it with an image of transparency, "an idea of a stream becoming thin: of seeing to the bottom."[6] The emptiness Peter feels is actually a "profound" insight into his deepest thoughts. In the second case, Peter appears to identify the bell with Clarissa (ll.18–19) but then imagines himself and Clarissa sitting in her family's country house at Bourton while the sound passes them by like a bee with honey.

Thus we have the sense of Clarissa as hostess (the narrator's implied personification) transformed into Clarissa at the mercy of a beelike hostess who takes away the "honey" of the moment. The image of Clarissa is compromised: she is the "tremor of delight" and the "moment of great intimacy," yet she is robbed of identity, dispersed, made impersonal by her association with sound and flight. She has achieved a surface poise but is virginal ("white" [l. 20]) in comparison with the natural, fecund imagery of the bee with honey that abandons her (l. 25). Her dance as society hostess seems unnatural and sterile.

When the cessation of the sound (l. 28) brings Peter back to his "sole self" (the mood of Keats's "Ode to a Nightingale" is appropriately evoked here), he realizes that the bells mark the passing moment, and he cannot rest with Clarissa's answer to life's transience, which is to spread herself among her friends. Clarissa's imagined "fall" (l. 32) seems to Peter to expose his "profound" (i.e., deep) happiness (l. 27) for what it really is: a deceptive surface as empty of real life as a skeleton is. He sees Clarissa's moments as contrived, artificial, and repetitious (the "skeleton of habit alone upholds the human frame" [ll. 3–4]); she falls, not necessarily dead, but spiritually dead, like a puppet when the show is over (Peter later describes London as a "show" just as Septimus calls the war the "whole show" [96]). Even Clarissa's moments have been robbed of their potency; Peter cannot exactly remember the room or the moment. In fierce reaction to the idea that even the skeleton is bound for dissolution, Peter commits himself to life and prepares to meet the breaking wave "rolling" (l. 35) toward him. Grief for the past and concern for the present are replaced by hope for the future.

Peter is indeed on his way to affirm his manhood by organizing the divorce for Daisy, his new love; more specifically, he will follow first the marching boys, then a pretty girl, up Whitehall. Unfortunately, he cannot keep up with the boys, and his "escapade" with the girl is a brief, unconsummated amusement.

Reading this passage is like sharing in the actual time during which Peter stands in the street. His initial paralysis is described in the first paragraph and is interrupted only by the first sounds of the clock: "Ah." As it peals, it "glides into the recesses of the heart" (56), although this suggestion of depth is countered by the following image of surface ripples, "ring after ring of sound" (we are reminded of Clarissa throwing her coin—her life—into the Serpentine). Like the moment, the sound is soon past, languishing, and Peter breaks out of his revery to live in the present. The bell of St. Margaret's mocks his nostalgia so that his grief at Clarissa's indifference to his visit is paradoxically comforted by that same indifference. He pushes once more on the seesaw of emotion, turning Clarissa's success into her fall, and his own fall (from that moment at Bourton when he almost married her) into a rising plunge into the future and what life may bring him. He realizes that Clarissa the society hostess has not "grown" since her Bourton days: her clock has stopped. He actually calls out, and begins to move. It may all have taken only a moment, but the sequence of details of that moment—the stream—is crucial, and precisely aligned.

THE STREAM OF CONSCIOUSNESS

Virginia Woolf is associated in people's minds with *stream of consciousness,* a phrase that originated in the pioneering psychological work of William James and Henri Bergson at the end of the nineteenth century and that points generally to an "entire area of mental attention,"[7] a subjective focus of interest in the novels of such writers as Dorothy Richardson, James Joyce, and Virginia Woolf. It is a useful starting point, and other expressions used to describe Woolf's technique, such as "psycho-analogy,"[8] are no more illuminating.

Humphrey distinguishes four types of this "stream": omniscient description, indirect interior monologue, direct interior monologue, and soliloquy. I have arranged these types in order of increasing independence from the narrator's voice. An example of all four types is seen in the following extract, in which Maisie Johnson, a visitor from Edinburgh, contemplates a life in London as she walks through Regent's Park:

> Horror! horror! she wanted to cry. (She had left her people; they had warned her what would happen.)
>
> Why hadn't she stayed at home? she cried, twisting the knob of the iron railing.
>
> That girl, thought Mrs Dempster (who saved crusts for the squirrels and often ate her lunch in Regent's Park), don't know a thing yet; and really it seemed to her better to be a little stout, a little slack, a little moderate in one's expectations. Percy drank. Well, better to have a son, thought Mrs Dempster. (31)

This passage begins as if it is a soliloquy (with echoes of Conrad's Kurtz from *Heart of Darkness,* whose dying words include "The horror!"), but we learn that it is only a thought wish—that is, a potential direct interior monologue. The parentheses in both paragraphs, as usual, contain omniscient description. "Why hadn't she stayed at home?" looks like direct speech but is in fact indirect, even though "she cried" appears forthrightly direct. We can tell that it is indirect by the lack of quotation marks, the use of the third person, and the employment of the pluperfect tense (direct speech would be, "Why didn't I stay at home?"). This technique of blurring the distinction between direct and indirect speech is common in Woolf and is part of her attempt to make the transitions between speech and thought as fluid and overlapping as they actually are in our subjective experience.

With Mrs. Dempster's speech we finally get direct interior monologue, "That girl don't know a thing." The fact that it is a monologue is signaled, as it often is in Woolf, by idiomatic use of language ("don't"). As Mrs. Dempster continues, the speech approaches soliloquy in its acknowledgment of an audience. In this case, Mrs. Dempster imagines speaking to Maisie directly. Even so, the narrator retains control by rendering part of the speech in indirect mode, for example, "it seemed to her" (cf. "it seems to me"), "Percy drank" (cf. "Percy drinks").

This passage illustrates a great advantage of the stream-of-consciousness style, which allows the narrator to slide in and out of a character's mind without interrupting the narrative flow. As Anne Banfield has shown (by comparing a passage of direct dialogue from "Mrs. Dalloway's Party" with its final indirect version in the novel[9] and by analyzing passages from the novel[10]), Woolf chose to inhabit this blurred mental landscape between soliloquy and omniscience so that the reader would experience contradictory rhythms: the seamless flow of the grammar of the prose versus the abrupt shifts in perspective from one character to another.

The novel as a whole, of course, repeats this sensation: at times it smoothly connects the disparate thoughts of unconnected inhabitants of London through shared public events and time; at other points, it shows their total separateness by misinterpretation, contrasting emotional moods, or gaps in the text. Using what Humphrey calls cutting, fade-out, and time and space montage in a cinematic way,[11] Woolf orchestrates individual speeches between past and present, interior thought and outward speech, and moves the reader between one character and another. Generally Woolf avoids identification with any authority and so creates a text as elusive as the old woman's song or the airplane's sign.

The passage analyzed earlier concerning Peter Walsh shows another feature of the sustained indirect monologue: it can give the reader the quality of a character's mind as we watch the character confirming or modifying ideas and sensations over time. As Barbara Hardy puts it, "Woolf uses the free indirect style to register the pressure and growth of feeling. She tears her characters out of their affective privacy, showing how passion is checked and qualified, as it gathers momentum and material from external sensations and events."[12] The stream is never simply a stream: it picks up and deposits material along its banks and sometimes carves new channels.

The challenge of the stream-of-consciousness technique, as Humphrey says, is for the writer who wishes to "depict what is chaotic (human consciousness at an inchoate level) while creating an ordered work of art."[13] This issue of control is complex. Critics of Woolf's style debate the degree of order she maintains over the "stream" of her characters' impressions. Close examination has shown that Woolf is in control of her prose throughout. Norman Page has analyzed the first sentences of *Mrs. Dalloway,* and concludes that it is "heavily patterned prose, hardly less so than that of Gibbon or Pater, with an extensive use of repetition of verbal structures, of balance and antithesis, of groupings in twos and threes, and with the arrangement of units of different lengths to create a definite climax. . . . Such prose possesses an *organized* quality which makes it essentially remote from truly spontaneous discourse."[14] This approach is far from the stream of consciousness that people sometimes think was pioneered by Woolf and that we might see more "naturally" in Molly Bloom's monologue at the end of *Ulysses.* Even in the monologues of Septimus, Woolf retains control of point of view and imagery; David Daiches says she had "a tidy mind" compared with that of Joyce.[15]

We can say, then, that Woolf presents "a studied element of incoherence"[16] within a controlled framework. Within the sentence, Woolf regularly uses signals for her psychological turns—for example, the nonspecific conjunction "for" and the slippage into the free-floating "one" halfway between first and third person (i.e., between interior monologue and omniscience).[17] On a more general level, as we move around individual minds in London the spatial dimension is ordered by the street names and such omniscient identifiers as "Peter said" or "Sally thought," while in the temporal dimension such events as the backfiring car, the chiming clocks, or various incidents at Bourton keep order.[18]

Woolf's view of an interconnected society fits well with current theories about semiotics and communication or its lack. It is a book full of messages: from the plane to the people, from Clarissa to Peter and vice versa, from Richard to Clarissa, from Lady Bruton to the *Times,* from Septimus to the world and to Holmes and Bradshaw, from the old woman at the tube station to . . . whom? Septimus's last words are "I'll give it you!" Give what to whom—a punch to Bradshaw, or a gift to Clarissa? Clarissa's message to Peter is "Come to my party." Does it mean, Come and talk to me, or rather, Come and don't talk to me? When we try to read the words in the world, whether we are examining our social institutions or listening to our partner, we find not a "stream" but gaps and contradictions. Like Clarissa and Septimus, we become aware that our reach exceeds our grasp. There is, however, the possibility that failed communication can spark other emotions: "the message hidden in the beauty of words . . . is loathing, hatred, despair" (98).

NARRATIVE CONTROL

Some critics find Woolf's control too insistent. Stuart Rosenberg, for example, after correctly observing that Woolf "shows the same love for her medium that Clarissa shows for life,"[19] goes on to object to the way Woolf calls attention "shrilly" to her art. He feels that Woolf is present as a character in the book as vividly as Peter Walsh or Richard Dalloway is, and this element annoys him. He shows how the narrator sometimes introduces her own images, or slips from a character's perspective to her own. These "artificial" devices are not confined to the mental imagery but extend to the very structure of the narrative. For example, Elise Mitchell is introduced as a character for a moment only, in order to run from the bench where Peter is dozing and crash into Rezia's legs (72–73). This linking device is certainly a rhetorical effect, similar to a camera tracking from one scene to another by means of a bird, or cat, or soccer ball. But it is not simply a crude seam in the fabric. Though the stream of consciousness has locks and flood-gates that the narrator quite openly manipulates throughout the novel, that manipulation has the effect of enacting in the reading process itself the contradictions and disjunctions Woolf felt in her society. Through *Mrs. Dalloway* Woolf is debating between her belief that our inner life *is* patterned and her observation that her society was divided, socially and politically.

Francis Gillen therefore includes the control of the novel as part of its purpose. He suggests that the reading experience of the novel parallels Clarissa's own efforts to discriminate between the rush of impressions, to find a point of balance on this side of reductive patterning: "That is what I find makes a novel by Virginia Woolf so deeply satisfying; it corresponds so closely to our own tenuous discovery of meaning through the experience of life itself. . . . [H]er novels are mimetic insofar as they not only contain meaning but imitate what was for Virginia Woolf the only viable way of apprehending that meaning without destroying growth, 'a system that did not shut out.' Meaning is tenuous in her novels because meaning is tenuous in life. Yet meaning is there."[20] Following a similar line, Geoffrey Hartman discusses the opening lines in terms of the gap, or "void," between plot and prose that encourages us to consider "two types of continuity": "The first line of the novel, 'Mrs Dalloway said she would buy the flowers herself,' presupposes some immediate prior fact already taken up in consciousness, a plot already set in motion, and is emblematic of the artist's mood throughout the novel. Our fascination is involved with this will to continuity, this free prose working under such strict conditions."[21]

Critics struggle to find an image that will adequately catch these two senses of freedom and necessity in Woolf's prose. E. M. Forster said the novel had "the framework of a summer's day, down which go spiralling two fates."[22] He also tried out the image of a cathedral (see chapter 3); he may have had in mind Woolf's own image of a butterfly's wing, or consciousness, resting on the monumental buttress or structure of a cathedral. Morris Philipson describes "an arabesque: a design of intertwined, interwoven elements that, starting from any one point of a geometrical or floral pattern, separate openly in order to conjoin at another point."[23] Reuben Brower sees the characters as connected "through a shuttling pattern of verbal reminiscences"[24] and describes "the exhilarated sense of being a part of the forward moving process and the recurrent fear of some break in this absorbing activity."[25] Hillis Miller identifies one of these patterns when he says, "If

Mrs. Dalloway is organized around the contrary penchants of rising and falling, these motions are not only opposites, but are also ambiguously similar."[26]

The degree to which readers feel Woolf's narrative control mirrors an actual system of connections in the real world finally depends on the degree to which they appreciate her mystical sense that life is fundamentally interconnected. It may be, as one critic has argued, that the very selflessness of the narrative is a feminist ideal, as reflected in the prose itself: "She lets grammar dissect and regulate the flow of the subject's desire, and keeps the conventional narrative form of third person and past tense. Within this apparent conformism, however, her writing tries to give voice to the specificity of a female subject who is outside any principle of identity-to-self, which can identify with multiple scenes without fully integrating herself into them."[27] But in this novel, I will suggest, Woolf's critique of England finally undermines the attempts of the narrator and Clarissa to bind up the wounds and see life whole, for there are times—most significantly in the three passages analyzed in chapter 6's section on feminism (but in fact percolating throughout the text)—when the narrator's strong opinions are put forward. These opinions interrupt the stream and rend the fabric of interconnections in both the text and the world of London.

PATTERNS

Time and Space

The novel contains nine major time divisions:

Time	Scenes	Minutes	Pages	Gaps
1. 10:00–11:00 A.M.	Clarissa shopping Septimus in park	60	5–33	—
2. 11:00–11:30 A.M.	Peter visits Clarissa	30	33–54	—

3. 11:30–11:45 A.M.	Peter walks to park		15	54–72	2
4. 11:45 A.M.– 12:00 noon	Septimus, Rezia, Peter		15	72–104	1
5. 12:00 noon– 1:30 P.M.	Bradshaw's consultation		90	104–113	—
6. 1:30–3:00 P.M.	Lady Bruton's lunch Richard returns home		90	113–136	—
7. 3:00–3:30 P.M.	Clarissa on Miss Kilman		30	136–140	—
8. 3:30–6:00 P.M.	Miss Kilman and Elizabeth Elizabeth's journey Septimus's suicide		150	140–167	—
9. 6:00 P.M.– 3:00 A.M.	Peter prepares for party Clarissa's party		540	167–215	2

As well as working through the day, the novel works around an area of central London so precisely that the characters' movements can be plotted on a map (see Figure 1). The significance of these spatiotemporal orderings is best described by working through them in terms of the nine divisions:

1. Clarissa's expedition takes her in a loop west and north from her home near Westminster Cathedral to the expensive shopping district of Bond Street. Here she and Septimus almost cross paths, since they are both interrupted by the ministerial car (Septimus's first description, significantly, is of one who "found himself unable to pass" [17]). Although they are part of the same nation, their paths do not literally cross, and Septimus and Rezia loop

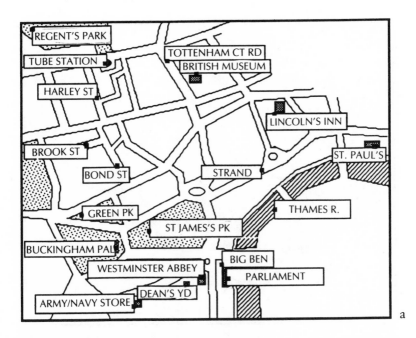

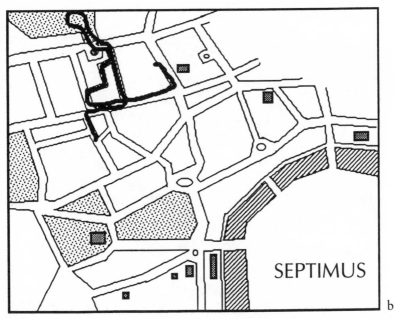

Figure 1. Maps of (a) Westminster and of the movement of (b) Septimus, (c) Clarissa, (d) Elizabeth, (e) Peter, and (f) Richard.

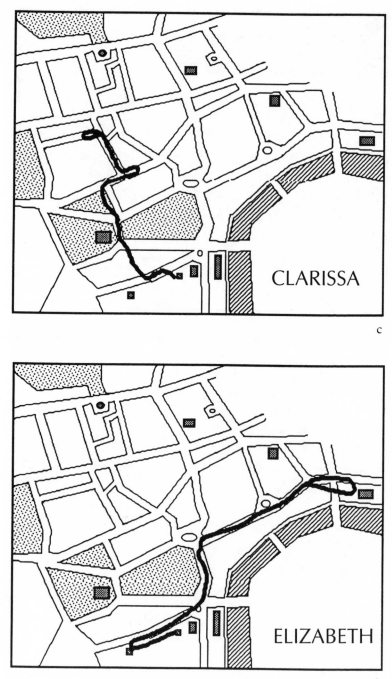

CLARISSA

c

ELIZABETH

d

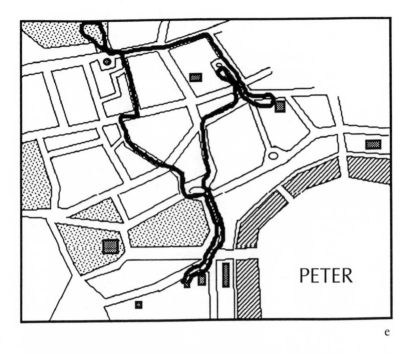

PETER

e

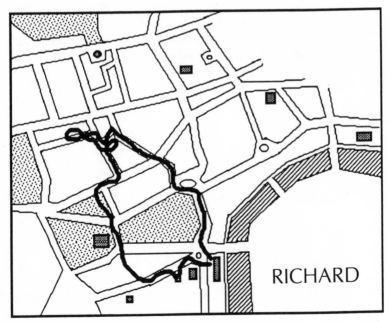

RICHARD

f

northward to Regent's Park while Clarissa returns home after walking into Brook Street, where her husband will later take lunch with Lady Bruton. The airplane, which links Septimus with many other Londoners, provides a connection across the first gap, since Clarissa, arriving home, comments, "What are they looking at?"

2. This section takes place entirely within Clarissa's house, although the announcement that Richard will be dining with Lady Bruton for lunch takes Clarissa's mind back over her life and loves. Peter Walsh's unexpected entrance continues and deepens those memories. At the end of the scene we leave the house with Peter.

3. Peter takes a fairly direct route northwest toward Regent's Park (he follows a girl across Piccadilly), where his memories of the past continue in the form of a dozing dream of women. This dream of the solitary traveler is set off by gaps (63, 65). He wakes out of a nightmare of being rejected by Clarissa.

4. Elise Mitchell provides the link in space between Peter's seat and the Smiths (72). The Smiths are about to walk to their appointment in Harley Street while Peter is busy rejecting his nostalgia in favor of the variety of the changed London he sees about him. Nevertheless, the challenge of the old woman at Regent's Park tube station, as he too leaves the park, suggests that detachment and domesticity are not the whole of life.

The old woman's song, like little Elise, provides another link across a gap to the next short section, in which Woolf outlines the history of the Smiths as they proceed to Harley Street by way of Portland Place.

5–7. The next three time sections, from noon to 3:30 P.M., are undivided and form the longest section in the novel. We begin with the Smiths' interview with Bradshaw; his rooms in Harley Street have taken them south toward the centers of power. We pass via the clocks of Harley Street to Lady Bruton's lunch (113) in Brook Street, even closer to the center, then follow Richard home to Clarissa (he and Hugh separate at Conduit Street). There we witness the confrontation between Clarissa and Miss Kilman, who is about to go out shopping with Elizabeth. The symmetry suggests we ask some searching questions. What, if anything, distinguishes the

Style

scenes between Richard and Lady Bruton and between Richard and Clarissa? What distinguishes Bradshaw from Miss Kilman, each the focus of a flanking scene?

8. One of the most complex transitions in the novel is found here. Clarissa moves from her immediate anger at the "odious Kilman" to a more general lament for destructive love. As the bells toll the half-hour, we move outside the house into the streets of London and into the mind of Miss Kilman, as she struggles to achieve Clarissa's apparent detachment.

Miss Kilman and Elizabeth walk westward along Victoria Street to the Army and Navy Stores. After tea, Elizabeth journeys east and north into the foreign country of London's legal and commercial district. In this undefined northeast district of London the power and the people are most at odds. Elizabeth's sentimental vision of England's military and imperial might modulates via the sun's rays into a perspective on Septimus's room off the Tottenham Court Road (154) and his last moments of happiness before his suicide. Compared with Dean's Yard, where the Dalloway house is a symbol of the soul's privacy, Septimus's room is open to invasion by the doctors and the public street, which a moment before was for Elizabeth a fantastical place of variety, liberation, and adventure.

9. The final section begins with the most ironic of crossovers, as Peter Walsh hears the ambulance on its way to the Smiths and thinks, "One of the triumphs of civilization" (167). We then follow Peter as he walks from the lawyer's office in Lincoln's Inn to his hotel in Bloomsbury, to the northeast. There he has dinner, then sets out for Clarissa's party. A gap takes us to the party itself and last-minute preparations. (182) The last gap in the text comes after Clarissa returns "from the little room" (206) and her meditation upon Septimus. Peter's innocuous remark, "But where is Clarissa?" is emphasized, since it begins the last section, and the reader is made to wonder just how much of Clarissa is in her party self. The question still remains in the last lines of the novel, when Peter's question is answered on a factual level ("For there she was") but remains a challenge to authentic living.

The focus of the novel is the Dalloway home in Dean's Yard, Westminster, but all the characters make forays north and east into the "real"

London. Clarissa compares her trivial action at the Serpentine (the pond in Hyde Park to the west) with Septimus's plunge, somewhere to the northeast in that part of London—that part of her mind—which she dares not explore. While both Richard and Peter come to Clarissa's house during the day, they journey away from it to the north with pleasure.

The clocks of London provide the obvious time scaffolding for the novel, but they go further than simply dividing the day into its hours or the novel into its nine sections. Big Ben conveys masculinity: the clock tower stands above the male-dominated Houses of Parliament, and even the name is phallic and male, and suggests the huge German gun "Big Bertha" that shelled Paris during the Great War. Its chimes leave "leaden circles" that "dissolve in the air." The "lead" suggests the gunfire that could be heard from the English coast, but the dissolving also suggests an opposite sense of delicacy and dissipation. The phrase is used four times in the novel, twice in parentheses, so that it becomes itself a familiar chime. Big Ben's remorseless order is softened not only by its dissolution but by the more feminine bells of St. Margaret's that follow it. Woolf on one occasion identifies this second clock with a sea wave bringing the flotsam of daily life to disturb the grand surface of the sea, "as if Big Ben were all very well with his majesty laying down the law, so solemn, so just, but she must remember all sorts of little things besides" (141).

This second clock is always female, in contrast to the authoritative male, and the reader tends to associate it with the passages of stream of consciousness and reminiscence. Clocks are what happen out there, in the streets, keeping order and signifying marches, commerce, and law. Inside houses, inside heads, is where St. Margaret the hostess moves softly, charmingly, chaotically. Woolf makes much of doorways and windows to emphasize this inner-outer life of people in a big city, at once public and private.

Two motions are thus established by Woolf's ordering of indoor/ outdoor scenes as well as by the characters' alternating between the happy present and the unhappy past: an emotional up and down, and a temporal forward and backward. (The Appendix concordance shows how often occur such words as *death, moment, life, old, time,* and *young.*) The reading rhythm is wavelike, as the leaden circles of fact and action dissolve in the air of imagination and reflection. The novel moves between these poles, creating a rhythm of emotional rising and falling identified by Maria DiBattista as "the source of the novel's exquisite suspense and excitement."[28]

There is also the suspicion that the emotional, structural, and historical center of it all is hollow, like a bell, a place of silence and death. At the first chime of the novel Clarissa is described as feeling "a particular hush, or solemnity; an indescribable pause; a suspense . . . before Big Ben strikes. There! Out it boomed" (6). But as she walks up Bond Street we are also told that "she had the oddest sense of being herself invisible; unseen; unknown; there being no more marrying, no more having of children now, but only this astonishing and rather solemn progress with the rest of them" (13). Here Clarissa is mimicking the "Royal Progress" that in former times the English monarch undertook through the realm. Her obedience to and worship of the monarchy are equated with the death of the self, with becoming "Mrs. Richard Dalloway." But the order of the British Empire symbolized by Big Ben has been broken; a passage shortly afterwards suggests why: " 'That is all,' she repeated, pausing for a moment at the window of a glove shop where, before the War, you could buy almost perfect gloves. And her old Uncle William used to say a lady is known by her shoes and her gloves. He had turned on his bed one morning in the middle of the War. He had said, 'I have had enough.' Gloves and shoes; she had a passion for gloves; but her own daughter, her Elizabeth, cared not a straw for either of them" (14). Here Woolf identifies Big Ben with the war itself; before its chime, all had been solemn and hushed, but now the old order has ended or "had enough." Despite her name, Elizabeth will not care for royalty as her mother does. This new postwar world is hard for Clarissa to read, as it is for the people watching the sign-writing plane. It is all "dissolved" and a person cannot "know" a woman by her clothes anymore. The clocks of London, then, which toll throughout the novel, are not simply structuring a single day. They are constant reminders of the division between past and present, between pre- and postwar Britain, and between the fairy-tale, Camelot world of Bourton and a present of compromise and loss.

Only Septimus escapes the bondage and pathos of clocks, because he has a far more apocalyptic sense of time. "I will tell you the time," he says to Evans, the dead man in the gray suit (79). Like T. S. Eliot, Septimus sees through the hollow men of London chained to their nine-to-five jobs. He would destroy it all and escape out of time into a promised land of brotherly love.

Motifs

In the section on narrative control there began to emerge two clusters of imagery, to which we might want to assign the names Clarissa and Septimus:

rise	fall
framework	spiral
order	disorder
progress	breakdown
joining	separation

But *Mrs. Dalloway* blurs these two categories with many other motifs.

One of the dominant motifs in the novel is war. It is everywhere, from the battlefields to the most trivial domestic incident. Even cigar smoke "breasted the air bravely" (63). Elizabeth guides Miss Kilman as if she were "an unwieldy battleship" in the "Army and Navy Stores" (143); Richard bears his flowers "like a weapon" (129); Ellie Henderson is in "a weaponless state" (186); Nature is "brandishing her plumes, shaking her tresses, flinging her mantle this way and that" (154); London "rushed her bayonets into the sky, pinioned her, constrained her to partnership in her revelry" (178–79).

Many other minor motifs serve to link the two main plots. For example, Peter feels that Clarissa works on his nerves (68), and shortly afterward Septimus feels "macerated until only the nerve fibers were left" (76); Peter notices the use of makeup in England (80), and again shortly afterward Septimus feels that people are "plastered over with grimaces" (99); Peter himself links Hugh ("indispensable to hostesses". [82]) with Clarissa, who has become "a mere hostess" (84). The people of London see the prime minister's car in the first pages, later Septimus wants to deliver his message to the prime minister, and finally Clarissa meets the prime minister at her party. Clarissa shops, Hugh shops; Peter and Septimus sit in Regent's Park; Clarissa and Rezia sew; Clarissa, Peter, and Septimus all weep; and so on.

City and country are constantly in opposition. Although at the beginning Clarissa confesses, "I love walking in London. . . . Really it's better than walking in the country" (8), Peter feels her natural setting is rural: "He saw her most often in the country, not in London" (170). Much of the action of the novel takes place in parks, which are oases of nature in the middle of a city. Even Bourton is remembered as a place of outdoors as much as indoors. The game of cricket is often mentioned (both Septimus and Peter scan the newspaper for the news of Surrey's performance in a county cricket match, and Holmes recommends the game to Septimus) because it is a game that is set symbolically in the countryside, on the village green, yet requires order, discipline, and mathematics.

Although the novel is set firmly in the heart of London, then, the city is closely linked with the pastoral. It seems from the first line to be filled with Nature: there are birds (jays, ducks, pouched birds, gulls, sparrows, canaries, rooks, swallows, birds of paradise); trees (elms, oaks, beeches, poplars); animals (ponies, dogs, cats, puppies, squirrels, Skye terriers, antelope, fox terriers, sea lions, geese, cattle, guinea pigs, salmon); plants (vegetables—cauliflowers, cabbages, cucumbers); and, of course, flowers (sweet peas, irises, roses, lilies, primroses, geraniums, hyacinths, crocuses, hollyhocks, dahlias, cow parsley, lilacs, camellias, delphiniums, orchids, rhododendrons, hibiscus lilies, syringas, blue hydrangeas). For a city novel there is also a bewildering array of natural settings, including sea, mists, swamps, and pampas grass.

Imagery of flowers and trees, in particular, arises naturally from the characters' activities. Woolf weaves her pastoral imagery around every character until her cast is like a garlanded circle celebrating the season. Clarissa feels part of "the trees at home" (11) and is usually dressed in green; she sees Daisy as "a lovely tree in the brisk sea-salted air of their intimacy" (51); Miss Kilman would like to "fell" Clarissa (138); Septimus, who had "flowered" into manhood before going to France, sees his wife as "a flowering tree" (163), as well as noticing a bird on a branch. There is a tree on the curtain of the prime minister's car, and Richard brings cut roses to Clarissa at lunch. Sally likes cutting the heads off flowers and floating them in a bowl; Rezia buys dying roses from a poor man (116); Lady Bruton poses with Hugh's red carnations (116); the crazed lady sings of love "like a wind-beaten tree for ever barren of leaves" (90). Trees are symbols of longevity and the earth; flowers are fragile, used to decorate city homes, and will die.

Woolf's references to Shakespeare's *Cymbeline* are not simply a literary overlay to tie Clarissa to Septimus before the party; they have an organic connection with this nature imagery. Clarissa recalls the words "Fear no more" four times during the day: once when she is shopping (she is looking in a bookshop window); once when she learns that Lady Bruton and Richard are dining together (jealousy quelled); once when sewing and remembering her youth with Peter (nostalgia quelled); and once as she contemplates Septimus's death (suicide quelled). Septimus recalls the same lines once, at his moment of contentment before Holmes comes to take him (154). In all these cases the lines suggest an emotion of security or philosophical surrender to fate, but at the same time the context ironically suggests the fragility of that security. This irony is there in the source: as Mark Hussey points out, the singers in *Cymbeline* are under a "double delusion," for although the dirge "Fear no more" is sung by Arviragus while he and his brother strew the "fairest flowers" to "sweeten thy sad grave" (act 4, scene 2, ll. 218–9), the victim is neither dead nor the boy Fidele (it is Imogen).[29] Perhaps the fear of death itself is a delusion, then—or perhaps, more usefully, we should recall that in both *Cymbeline* and *Mrs. Dalloway* a "dead boy" betokens a live woman.

The larger context of the allusion might also, as I have argued elsewhere,[30] show us how to pattern all this natural imagery into a political theme. Shakespeare's singers will soon be discovered as future rulers of England. The prophecy of Jupiter in the play reads, "When from a stately cedar shall be lopp'd branches which, being dead many years, shall after revive, be jointed to the old stock, and freshly grow, then shall Posthumus end his miseries, Britain be fortunate, and flourish in peace and plenty" (act 5, scene 4, ll. 140–5). There are many falling trees in *Mrs. Dalloway*: Clarissa's sister Sylvia (a word meaning "wood") was killed by a falling tree ("all Justin Parry's fault—all his carelessness" [87]); Septimus warns against cutting down trees, but he himself falls, a felled tree. Is he then the diseased branch, lopped off for the sake of Britain's health? Is Clarissa's party a thing of cut flowers, moments that may seem fleeting and artificial (like Clarissa's green gown, which fades in the sunlight) but that are the paradoxical signs of immortality and continuance? Certainly the state of England, in this novel, is to be determined to some degree botanically.

In her introduction to the American Modern Library edition of the novel (1928), Woolf suggests how we might combine these two images of trees and flowers. She describes books as "the flowers of fruit stuck here and there on a tree which has its roots deep down in the earth of our earliest life."[31] Flowers stand for the private life of emotion, such as the moment Clarissa experiences in the florist's shop; trees stand for the subconscious and its image in social institutions, such as the image on the gray blind of the car out in the street. Clarissa stands for the tree of state, but that state has been responsible for the felling of a generation of saplings. Are her flowers, then, not the natural reproductive organ of the vegetable world but, rather, tokens of grief strewn on the wooden coffin of a dying civilization?

Surface and Depth

Flowers stand for surface, and tree roots for depth. Near the end of the novel Peter observes, "Having done things millions of times enriched them, though it might be said to take the surface off" (180). In modern society, "surface" or "gloss" have a deprecatory association of insincerity and shallowness, yet Clarissa seems to love surfaces. When she is told of Richard's lunch with Lady Bruton, she feels "as she stood hesitating one moment on the threshold of her drawing-room, an exquisite suspense, such as might stay a diver before plunging while the sea darkens and brightens beneath him, and the waves which threaten to break, but only gently split their surface, roll and conceal and encrust as they just turn over the weeds with pearl" (34–35). When she looks in the mirror she sees herself as a diamond surface, composed—"one woman who sat in her drawing-room and made a meeting-point . . . had tried to be the same always, never showing a sign of all the other sides of her" (42). Later, when Peter recalls the way she jilted him, he remembers "grinding against something physically hard; she was unyielding. She was like iron, like flint, rigid up the backbone" (72). This jeweler's image of Clarissa as sparkling but cold may allow her different "facets" but remains an image of surfaces.

For many in London society, surfaces are safety. Hugh Whitbread "did not go deeply. He brushed surfaces" (114); but Lady Bradshaw had unfortunately gone under—so had Lady Bruton (126). What depths conservative society does allow involve communal feelings of patriotism, felt, for example, when the car passes along the street and leaves a ripple: "For the surface agitation of the passing car as it sunk grazed something very profound" (21).

But just as the nature imagery becomes problematic, so do the surfaces and depths begin to exchange values in the novel, depending on one's point of view. Peter Walsh has a complex notion of depths and surfaces, and moves between the two. At one moment he feels "sucked up to some very high roof by that rush of emotion, and the rest of him, like a white shell-sprinkled beach, left bare" (168). At another, he muses: "For this is the truth about our soul . . . our self, who fish-like inhabits deep seas and plies among obscurities threading her way between the boles of giant weeds, over sun-flickered spaces and on and on into gloom, cold, deep, inscrutable; suddenly she shoots to the surface and sports on the wind-wrinkled waves; that is, has a positive need to brush, scrape, kindle herself, gossiping" (178). Here the surface is associated with friction and flame but also with trivia. The depths are associated with threading and calm connection but also with cold inscrutability.

Despite these qualifications and Woolf's admiration for Clarissa's social skills, there is a sense that it is necessary to confront and understand one's psychological depths. The Septimus subplot literally "adds depth" to Clarissa's day. In *A Room of One's Own* Woolf describes the new psychological territory that the woman writer might explore: "she will light a torch in that vast chamber where nobody has yet been. It is all half lights and profound shadows like those serpentine caves where one goes with a candle peering up and down, not knowing where one is stepping."[32] This quotation gives new meaning to Clarissa's feeling that she had once thrown a coin into the Serpentine, for she, unlike Septimus, has not dared to explore those depths which she knows exist.

Webs and Waves

Critics of *Mrs. Dalloway* often select one dominant image to describe its achievement: the web. Brower writes of "shuttles" and David Daiches of "the weaving present and the woven past,"[33] Rosenberg describes Woolf "spinning" a character's vision out of her own,[34] and Geoffrey Hartman's article "Virginia's Web" describes the "rich prose woven by Clarissa's mind."[35]

The idea of spinning connections is implicit from the first page. It is a way of connecting past and present, as Clarissa connects the June morning with the past, a day at Bourton. The air was, and is, like "the flap of a wave"; this image suggests that the sea is the common element uniting moments, or waves. (This image was one Woolf used to structure a whole novel, *The Waves* [1931].) By page 9 the wave has become identified with the "divine vitality" that Clarissa senses throughout London, in the air and in every leaf. In biological terms, the connecting substance is sunlight or water; in terms of weaving, it is the thread of the tapestry itself.

In the opening scene we might think that the organic image applies to Clarissa's very senses, as she responds to the smells and sights of the London streets. Her holistic view extends beyond the body to the body politic, the community she belongs to and helps maintain. This connection between the individual body and something transcending the individual is crucial to Clarissa's spiritual beliefs, as it was (as we have seen) to Woolf, and yet it remains "interwoven" with the details of here and now. Woolf combines the wave image, with which she began, and the nature imagery, which will dominate the novel, as follows: "[d]id it not become consoling to believe that death ended absolutely? but that somehow in the streets of London, on the ebb and flow of things, here, there, she survived, Peter survived, lived in each other, she being part, she was positive, of the trees at home; of the house there, ugly, rambling all to bits and pieces as it was; part of people she had never met; being laid out like a mist" (11–12). Clarissa herself has become that connecting medium, not air but a "mist between the people she knew best, who lifted her on their branches as she had seen the trees lift the mist, but it spread ever so far, her life, herself" (12). Here the image of the wave has been transformed into a wave of energy (perhaps the process of photosynthesis itself, for this is a very "green" novel) that spreads out through space. The microcosm—the veins of a single leaf—has become the macrocosm of a forest covering England and perhaps the world. Each twig in the forest (Clarissa has just recalled how she knows only a few "twigs" of facts) is a filament carrying the fluid vitality of life itself.

Woolf unites and animates London through this imagery of connection and vibration. Whereas trees and flowers, surfaces and depths, tend to become oppositional patterns of imagery, the web remains a positive, connecting force. The prime minister's car leaves a "ripple" as it passes; bells and sparrows' calls resonate through the air to every corner; the playful dogs are "washed over" by the soft warm air (30). The image of spinning leads to spiders. Richard Dalloway and Hugh Whitbread feel "connected" as they leave Lady Bruton's lunch, their "thin thread" (124) of attachment trailing behind as they crawl like spiders across Westminster, until at the jewelers' Richard cuts the thread tying him with Hugh and Lady Bruton, and leaps like an acrobat to another. He sets out "to travel that spider's thread of attachment between himself and Clarissa" (127).

Near the end of the novel, as evening approaches, Woolf combines all three patterns—spider, wave, and mesh—by describing the

Bedford Square, September 1931. From Steen Eiler Rasmussen, *London: The Unique City* (London: Jonathan Cape, 1937), 193.

streets of London as the waterways of Venice. People setting off for evening functions are like water boatmen: "Whitehall was skated over, silver beaten as it was, skated over by spiders" (181). Peter imagines our deepest self is a fish "threading her way between the boles of giant weeds" (178) until it shoots to the surface from a need to "brush, scrape, kindle herself, gossiping."

The trick of living well lies in the ability to balance surface and depth living. In terms of the web, one must balance between following the line of others and spinning a line for oneself in order to drop down vertically into individuality. Septimus obviously cannot maintain his balance at the surface. His web is vertical rather than horizontal; because he slices reality differently, he does not fit into the system. As his wife cried he "descended another step into the pit" (100), and he escapes forever the demands of surface living by "plunging" vertically out the window. There is irony in his fall, of course, as well as a pun in the gruesome manner of his death. Attempting to live in depth, Septimus is impaled on "Mrs. Filmer's area railings" (165). Those "railings" signify both the territorial boundaries of urban living that separate neighbor from neighbor and the "railings of a madman" that Septimus has uttered all day, in an effort to reach out to other human beings.

As the social and psychological web is threatened by violence (the memory of war still pervades the streets of London like a lingering virus), so, too, is the prose texture threatened by images of violence as if by depth charges. Consider the high occurrence of words like *war, dead, death,* and *horror* in the novel, or the following motifs from just the first sixty pages:

- Clarissa "bursting" and "plunging" (5)
- Big Ben's "leaden circles" (6)
- people "tramping, trudging" (6)
- Clarissa "battling" through the night with the spectral Miss Kilman (15)
- a "pistol shot" in the street outside (16)
- men ready to "attend their Sovereign, if need be, to the cannon's mouth" (21)

- "the retreat from Moscow" (35–36)
- horses pawing the ground "before a battle begins" (50)
- "the brandishing of silver-flashing plumes" (52)
- marching "boys in uniform, carrying guns" (57)

PAINTING AND STRUCTURE

Woolf was keenly interested in the connections between writing and painting. She learned about the theory of composition from her friend Roger Fry's passion for the postimpressionists. A look at Seurat's *La Grande Jatte* or Cézanne's *Bathers* will show how those painters tried to impose shape on an ordinary scene through color, light, and form. Woolf began experimenting with significant form in her early short stories. "Kew Gardens," for example, is a painting in prose, a worm's-eye view of various couples out strolling in the gardens on a Sunday afternoon.

In 1922 she wrote to a friend, "One must . . . renounce finally the achievement of the greater beauty: the beauty which comes from completeness. . . . [B]eauty is only got by the failure to get it; by grinding all the flints together."[36] Clearly Woolf was prepared to be as daring as the postimpressionist painters in creating new forms of art in her novels, which were not, at first reading, beautiful. With *Mrs. Dalloway* Woolf said she had to "wrench" her substance to fit her "queer and masterful" design, and so it was obviously crucial to her to have such a design. She was corresponding with Jacques Raverat about the subject during the composition of the novel, and in 1925 she told him she was a kind of painter: "I rather think you've broached some of the problems of the writers too, who are trying to catch and consolidate and consummate . . . those splashes of yours." Woolf's biographer concludes, "She is claiming for herself the ability, or at least the intention, to see events out of time, to apprehend processes of thought and feeling as though they were pictorial shapes."[37]

Obviously *Mrs. Dalloway* is very much a matter of perspectives and the arrangement of large blocks of material. As David Daiches puts it, the basic theme is "the relation of loneliness to love,"[38] and he shows how the concerns of the individual (personal history and personal relations) interact with the concerns of the community (national history and London society). In an attempt to diagram how the novel moves, Daiches signifies the characters by letters and memories by *T* (more distant memories are *T1*, etc.).[39] Another diagram offered by Nancy Topping Bazin brings out clearly the "Ping-Pong" movement of the plot.[40] (See Figures 2 and 3.) But a more useful image for Woolf's "painting" process might be one that operates in a third dimension. "The tunnelling process"—the metaphor Woolf used for her writing at this time—ties together the strands of illumination and the ordinary with structure. It suggests surfaces and depths as well as archaeology, digs in chosen places. As Edward Hungerford notes, Woolf also used the tunneling image in her art criticism at this time. Of her sister Vanessa's paintings Woolf said that they yield their meaning only to those who "tunnel their way behind the canvas into masses and passages and relations and values of which we know nothing."[41]

How can the novelist suggest those depths which are beyond even the moments of epiphany often experienced by Woolf's characters? Woolf does it through the temporal reading process itself. She was at this time fascinated by the process of aesthetic apprehension, particularly of spatial art. As she described it in a 1925 essay, "Pictures," beneath the sensory impressions of a scene "our minds are tunnelling logically and intellectually into the obscurity of the young man's emotions, which as they ramify and modulate and stretch further and further, at last penetrate too far, peter out into such a shred of meaning that we can scarcely follow any more, were it not that suddenly in flash after flash, metaphor after metaphor, the eye lights up that cave of darkness and we are shown the hard tangible material shapes of bodiless thoughts hanging like bats in the primeval darkness where light has never visited them before."[42] Obviously Septimus's thoughts are like these flashes: disconnected metaphors from the deep subconscious that occasionally make conscious sense. But perhaps daily living also connects, in this fitful way. The old woman opposite Clarissa becomes a batlike figure, an emanation of Clarissa's own unknown mind that she

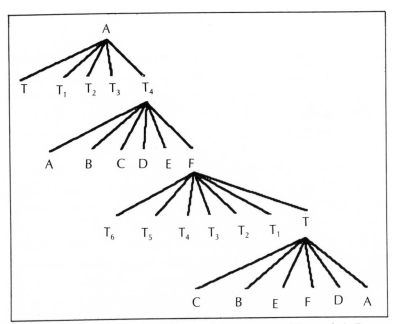

Figure 2. Here David Daiches has diagrammed the movement of the novel: A–F represent the characters; T represents the novel's present action; and T_1, T_2, T_3, etc., represent past moments. Reproduced by permission from David Daiches, *The Novel and the Modern World* (Chicago: University of Chicago Press, 1960), 212.

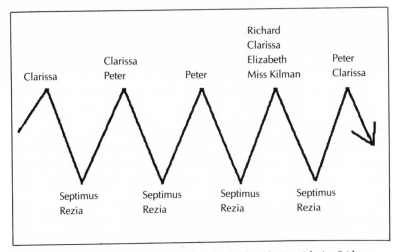

Figure 3. Nancy Bazin here represents by lines the "eight sights" or "devices" (the motor car, the airplane, the running child, the clock, the woman singing, the clock, the omnibus, the ambulance) that connect the two worlds of the novel. Reproduced by permission from Nancy Topping Bazin, *Virginia Woolf and the Androgynous Vision* (New Brunswick, N.J.: Rutgers University Press, 1973), 115.

encounters for a moment and barely recognizes. It is herself she sees, alone. But Clarissa's ability is to connect and raise up the caves, translating her own batlike thoughts into the clear light of the party rooms and making all surface. Clarissa's deepest fears of life's meaninglessness she immediately reinterprets as evidence of the variety of London life. The connection she makes is entirely horizontal and social, from one room to another. We may recall that for Woolf, London's streets "took up" the private life and carried it on, preventing it from settling. So Clarissa translates the subterranean network of caves and passages into the clear light of day, and Septimus's symbolic telegrams into the chitchat of party conversation with Bradshaw. In contrast, Peter Walsh's thoughts "peter" out in the mental depths, full of unconnected rooms with their impulses of regret, passion, and failure.

If we think of the narrator of *Mrs. Dalloway* as a painter, she is someone busily brushing over the cracks in her canvas, blurring the joins so as to give the impression of a seamless whole. If we look closer we see nothing but oppositions, some of which I have discussed here; and if we look even closer, the whole edifice starts to look shaky and to fall apart, undermined by the narrator's tunnels and by the subconscious tunnels of her characters. Reading the novel is more like taking a walk in the fields or "corridors" (as Woolf put it) than taking a stroll down the paved and orderly sidewalks of Bond Street. At any moment a pothole, slip, or detour will make us aware of the effort required to compose and hold together this June day. Between sentences, paragraphs, and sections there loom chasms, black holes.

The unifying force comes from three equally unsatisfactory sources. The first is Clarissa herself, gushing from the first page with her excitement about the present moment. The second is Septimus, with his apocalyptic vision of a world that must be made new, at once. In both cases, according to Maria DiBattista, their style of "unbroken sequentiality . . . issues out of an undeniable morbidity, a contagious emanation from the febrile temper of its 'heroine,' recently afflicted with influenza, and of Septimus Smith, victimized by a darker pathology. . . . Only a continuous style could tranquilize the narrative susceptible to such sudden and erratic perturbations."[43]

The nurse administering the tranquilizer is the narrator, the third possible source of unity and a significant form; but the narrator, as we have seen, organizes the novel only in terms of contraries and shifting oppositions.

Despite the patterning in the novel, then, it remains essentially disorganized, as Woolf works against her natural synthetic tendency. Woolf may have written in "Mr. Bennett and Mrs. Brown" that a writer must be like a "hostess" bridging the gulf to the reader,[44] but in *Mrs. Dalloway* she does much more than pass the tray and describe the weather on this fine day in June. The patterns of her imagery work against her shifting syntax to create the contradictory fabric of her world. The novel therefore provides the reader with an absorbing and challenging reading experience, through its use of stream of consciousness and patterns of imagery and through the juxtapositions of the present with the past and Clarissa's story with Septimus's. The text oscillates rhythmically between memories and this day in June, between the preparation for a party and the party itself, between analysis and synthesis, private experiences and things shared, self and society.

While Woolf wanted to reflect accurately a divided postwar world, she also wanted to resist the temptation to take over the male position of *author*ity. We have discussed this tension in relationship to the stream-of-consciousness technique and narrative control. As one critic puts it, "The complicity of writing with established power is the suppressed, never fully realized sub-text of *Mrs. Dalloway*, the source of the novel's deep and unresolved ambivalence towards its own representational activity."[45] We will pursue this idea in chapter 6's section on feminism.

6

Characters and Themes

CLARISSA DALLOWAY, NÉE PARRY

Clarissa Dalloway

> *Fifty-two years old. Daughter of Justin Parry, niece of Helena Parry, who wrote a book on the orchids of Burma. In the 1890s Clarissa lived in the family country home at Bourton, where her sister, Sylvia, was killed by a falling tree. There she met Sally Seton; Peter Walsh; and Richard Dalloway, whom she married. She has a "pea-stick figure" and a "bird beak." She lives in Westminster. She has recently been ill with influenza but enjoys giving parties.*

In the 1920s Virginia Woolf wrote a memoir for her friends and family, recalling her childhood as the daughter of Sir Leslie Stephen, philosopher, editor, and literary critic. The family members lived in a large house in central London, and theirs was a world of books and balls. It was Woolf's mother, Julia (née Duckworth), who remained a source of fascination and puzzlement to Woolf, an "invisible presence" that obsessed her until the mother's ghost was "laid" (as Woolf put it) in *To the Lighthouse,* the novel she wrote after *Mrs. Dalloway.* In the first decades of the twentieth century Woolf was engaged in a pro-longed meditation on her mother's character and world.

There is already much of Julia in Clarissa Dalloway. Julia was an efficient and devoted wife, a woman whom Virginia recalled as "impetuous, and also a little imperious; so conscious of her own burning will that she could scarcely believe that there was not something quicker and more effective in her action than in another's."[1] Julia was thirty-six when Virginia was born, and she died when Virginia was just thirteen. Woolf noted her mother's exhaustion at running a large family in a large house, how she "sank, like an exhausted swimmer" (an image that evokes Lady Bradshaw "going under"), but also her vitality and magnetism. Julia was constituted, Woolf argues, by her setting and by those around her (Clarissa feels her identity is spread out among her friends): "When we exclaim at the extravagant waste of such a life we are inclined no doubt to lose that view of her surrounding parts, the husband and child and home, which if you see them as a whole surrounding her, completing her, robs the single life of its arrow-like speed, and its tragic departure."[2]

While Julia seemed central to everything, she was also emotionally distant. This is the price of spreading oneself: "she was keeping what I call in my shorthand the panoply of life—that which we all lived in common—in being."[3] The word *panoply* is a military image Woolf uses in *Jacob's Room* to describe the everyday paraphernalia (another military word) of life, and in *Mrs. Dalloway* to describe Clarissa's "panoply of content" (15). The word suggests the fight these women waged on the "home front" to maintain civility and order.

There is no question that Woolf believed in the value of waging this war to maintain civilization at home, even at the level of class values. In another memoir, "Am I a Snob?" (1936), she frankly admits, "If you ask me would I rather meet Einstein or the Prince of Wales, I plump for the Prince without hesitation."[4] She concludes that she is a thorough snob—a "social festivity snob" and a "coronet snob"—and it is easy to imagine that she would feel the same quiver of delight and awe that Clarissa feels, at the beginning of the novel, about the prime minister's car and, at the end, when her party begins.

It is generally accepted that Clarissa Dalloway was modeled on a friend of the Stephen family, Kitty Maxse. According to Woolf's biographer, Maxse was "smart, with a tight, neat pretty smartness; her blue eyes looked at the world through half-closed lashes; she had a lovely mocking voice; she stood very upright."[5] Woolf herself recalls Maxse as having "the reputation of profound knowledge and exquisite sympathy."[6] On 4 October 1922, as noted in chapter 4, Kitty Maxse apparently fainted, fell over a banister, and died.[7]

Clarissa may have a variety of more distant originals than Woolf's immediate family and friends. Jane Marcus suggests that Woolf was familiar with the work of her aunt Caroline Stephen, in particular her history *The Service of the Poor* (1871). There Caroline Stephen described the Clarissans, the third order of St. Francis, women who married but were celibate, who cared for the poor and insane secretly— outsiders caring for outsiders.[8] Woolf also used the name Clarissa in her letters to refer to the unborn child of Vanessa, of whom Virginia was thinking when she was in a mental home convalescing from her emotional illness, one of the consequences of which was that she was persuaded (as I said in chapter 4) not to have children.[9] Woolf was also familiar with Samuel Richardson's *Clarissa,* that victim of the aristocracy who learned to beat the system by joining it.

From this cluster of sources we might expect that Woolf's attitude toward Clarissa Dalloway would be a mixture of scorn and admiration, the harsh attitude tinged with an understanding of the sacrifice required, particularly of family and fame, to maintain sanity and society. Certainly the portrayal of Clarissa in *The Voyage Out* is harsh. If Clarissa's husband in *The Voyage Out* is a prurient male chauvinist, his wife is not much better. Morris Philipson says, "A reader's judgment of her self-conscious fragility, her passivity, her society worldliness may actually be negative, and one's associations with her name might suggest a Callow-way or Shallow-way."[10] Clarissa is introduced as a sentimental patriot. In Lisbon she photographed Fielding's grave and let loose a small bird that some ruffian had trapped, " 'because one hates to think of anything in a cage where English people lie buried,' [Clarissa's] diary stated" (39). Like her husband, Clarissa sails in from another century, indeed she looks like "an eighteenth-century masterpiece—a Reynolds or a Romney" (47). She tells Rachel that she loves Richard not only because he is "clean" (50) but also because he is androgynous and brings out the best in her: "When I was your age I wanted too. No one understood until I met Richard. He gave me all I wanted. He's man and woman as well. . . . What one wants in the person one lives with is that they should keep one at one's best" (65).

Clarissa's sexless vivacity is undiscriminating, and she does not need to caution herself, because she belongs to the power group and the world is her oyster. Blithely can she say, "But after all . . . *everyone's* interesting really" (42). Only Helen Vinrace cuts through Clarissa's smothering, hypocritical enthusiasm for life's variety. An example follows this speech by Clarissa:

> "When I'm with artists I feel so intensely the delights of shutting oneself up in a little world of one's own, with pictures and music and everything beautiful, and then I go out into the streets and the first child I meet with its poor, hungry, dirty little face makes me turn round and say, 'No, I *can't* shut myself up—I *won't* live in a world of my own. I should like to stop all the painting and writing and music until this kind of thing exists no longer.' Don't you feel," she wound up, addressing Helen, "that life's a perpetual conflict?"
> Helen considered for a moment. "No," she said. (45)

At the beginning of *Mrs. Dalloway* Clarissa seems to be equally uncritical in her celebration of London. This exhilaration with the metropolis, or rather with the general impression of "life . . . this moment," was familiar to Woolf herself. In her diary of January 1918 Woolf wrote:

> I drove on top of a Bus from Oxford St. to Victoria Station, & observed how the passengers were watching the spectacle: the same sense of interest & mute attention shown as in the dress circle before some pageant. A Spring night; blue sky with a smoke mist over the houses. The shops were still lit . . . & in Bond Street I was at a loss to account for a great chandelier of light at the end of the street; but it proved to be several shop windows jutting out into the

road. . . . The gentleness of the scene was what impressed me; a twilight view of London. Houses very large & looking stately. Now & then someone, as the moon came into view, remarked upon the chance for an air raid.[11]

During the longer time span of the novel, Woolf introduces a feeling of unease in both Clarissa and the reader by splitting the screen, so to speak, and exposing one of the casualties of that English pageant to our unwilling gaze. In many ways Clarissa is sympathetic to Septimus's anguish. She too is suspicious of absolutists like Bradshaw and Miss Kilman. Blackstone goes so far as to say, "If only she could have met Rezia and Septimus in the Park, we tell ourselves regretfully, she would certainly have spoken to them (as Peter realized), she would have protected them and Sir William would not have got near them."[12] Clarissa and Septimus share many personal qualities. While choosing extreme examples of sexual roles, the soldier and the hostess, Woolf shows Septimus to be sensitive, imaginative, and emotional, happy to be at home with his wife, who is the breadwinner, while Clarissa is shown to be a fighter and a thinker as well as a wife and mother. Indeed, her affinities with Septimus begin on the first page, with her "solemn" sense of the hours. This communal sense of the moment recalls soldiers' descriptions of the twice-daily stand-to and stand-down at the front, so regular with both armies that "there was attaching to it a degree of *solemnity,* in that one was conscious that from the sea dunes to the mountains, everywhere, on the whole front the two opposing lines stood alertly, waiting any eventuality"[13] (emphasis added).

Of course, Clarissa is compromised. For all her sympathy, the grotesque situation in the trenches was the logical extension of something she regarded as noble: blind obedience, suppression of self, even of logic, for the sake of one's homeland. This alignment of Clarissa with the worst excesses of the war—moreover, with being insincere and playing a part or "being at one's best"—is a continuation of the Clarissa of *The Voyage Out* and "Mrs. Dalloway in Bond Street."

But the later Clarissa, as I have been suggesting, is a more complex and sympathetic character. Whenever her social function is mentioned it must be qualified by her love of life, particularly when she is being judged by her most astute critic, Peter Walsh. If she gives parties "for her idea of Richard" (86), if she maintains a network of visitors, calling cards, and good works, it is, Peter recognizes, done "from a natural instinct" (86). Clarissa's own answer comes later, when she ponders Peter and Sally's criticism that she is a snob who enjoys "imposing herself" through her class and her parties: "And both were quite wrong. What she liked was simply life. 'That's what I do it for,' she said, speaking aloud to life" (134).

As the political critique of the novel sharpens, so this sense strengthens that Clarissa's enthusiasm for life is more than city hype. At the outset we might see Clarissa as playing the part of someone in *The Voyage Out;* it is her party world that is the fantasy, not Septimus's feelings. But we learn that her parties are her sincere "offering" to a religion of life. Once, in an omnibus with Peter, she had explained her "transcendental theory" about how "our apparitions, the part of us which appears, are so momentary compared with the other, the unseen part of us, which spreads wide . . . [that] the unseen might survive, be recovered somehow attached to this person or that, or even haunting certain places, after death" (169). Clarissa's parties are rituals where this immortalizing process might happen, where people might spread themselves among other people, to weave themselves into the enduring fabric. Like her creator, Clarissa articulates a mystical theory of pattern and connection.

Clarissa's breadth of acquaintance is matched by a breadth of imagination. Because we are used to the dominance of the inner life in a Woolf novel, we perhaps forget how remarkably alive is Clarissa's mind, how free and untrammeled her consciousness. Woolf takes pains to establish Clarissa as a philosopher: "her favorite reading as a girl was Huxley and Tyndall" (86). In her confrontation with Miss Kilman we see Clarissa's intellect to best advantage. At first she dismisses Miss Kilman for being of a lower class (139), her plain physical appearance a physical analogue for her thuggish doctrine of conversion through "love and religion." Clarissa refines her idea by watching the woman in the room opposite and concluding that neither Peter Walsh nor Miss Kilman would be able to solve that "miracle," that "mystery" (141). Clarissa is not thinking of fashionable dress and makeup when she objects to Miss Kilman's appearance. She has in mind a subtler idea of how one presents oneself to others in society, the kind of acknowledgment of one's own and others' individuality that Miss Kilman would deny by putting everyone in a uniform of mackintoshes. Clarissa treasures the kind of everyday difference symbolized by the clock that chimes after Big Ben's "law" and that suggests "all sorts of little things" (141). It is therefore Miss Kilman's uniqueness, her attempt to be theoretical while at the same time muttering, "It is the flesh" and impetuously buying a petticoat, that compels Clarissa to love as well as hate her, for Miss Kilman *is* an individual full of contradictions, try as she might to be a theory.

On the darker side of Clarissa's response to life is an existential confrontation with its absurdity, the "terror . . . the fear" (204). There are many moments during her day (such as when she learns that Richard is lunching with Lady Bruton) when she seriously questions everything she and Richard stand for. Unable to "reach the center," as she puts it, she averts her eyes from this cold core and, like the phoenix, rises birdlike from Richard's protective nest in party after party, "rubbing stick to stick" and person to person and revealing her "best" self. This "offering" is quite consciously utilitarian, a way of avoiding her acute awareness of mortality: "After that, how unbelievable death was!" (135)

Clarissa's attempt to break down the barriers of polite conventionality and make contact with people is in part a substitute for a full sexual life. While Richard rushes home with flowers, we see little during the day of a warm emotion from Clarissa for her husband. As one critic observes, "Clarissa is both perfectly conventional in her role as lady and hostess and, at the same time, a misfit: *Mrs. Dalloway* is all about the fact that she is still unresolved in a choice apparently completed a generation before."[14] The importance of Clarissa's decision to follow social custom, abandon her lesbian love for Sally, and marry Richard is revealed in the way she responds to the death of

Septimus. Clarissa instinctively recalls her moments with Sally at Bourton, the link being the quotation from *Othello* (39, 204). Clarissa had once "come down . . . in white" (204); now Septimus has come down, onto the railings. At Bourton Clarissa continued down the stairs and sat beside Richard rather than Sally; in contrast, Septimus, she hopes, "plunged holding his treasure," refusing to compromise his passion to social pressures. But society is exactly what has murdered Septimus's spirit, whether through the war itself or through the medical profession's (mis)treatment of him. This idea is symbolized in his last moments. Just before he jumped, Septimus saw an old man coming down a staircase, a figure who stopped and stared at him (165). When Clarissa looks across at the room opposite, she too sees a figure, a single woman going to bed alone. In these two moments both characters see themselves and the lonely future to which they have been sentenced. In *A Room of One's Own* Woolf recounted seeing from her London window a man and woman getting into a taxi.[15] This scene, she felt, symbolized the two sexes that reside within each of us and that must live in harmony if we are to live wholly. Both Septimus and Clarissa look out at solitary individuals of their own sex, suggesting that both characters have rejected their own sexuality. (Septimus's homosexuality is discussed in the next section.) Woolf makes it clear, through Clarissa's involvement with Sally and Septimus's with Evans, that one's sexual nature may be manifested in either homosexual or heterosexual relationships. What matters is that it be manifested, and Clarissa and Septimus have chosen celibacy.

Yet Clarissa's decision to replace Sally with Richard is reasonable, particularly when contrasted not with Sally but with the exhausting intensity that a life with Peter might have involved. Clarissa's self-extension through the space of London high society is a fully conscious choice, based on the dangers of self-absorption that accompany sexual passion and fulfillment in depth. Reference is twice made to Constantinople, an exotic location where, presumably, Clarissa responded frigidly to Richard's advances. Yet she still manages to excite and satisfy him: holding her hand, he thinks, "Happiness is this" (132).

Clarissa's greater triumph is her party. For DiBattista, Clarissa is in league with the feminine "law-giver" in honoring privacy, virginity, and individuality, while at the same time providing a social meeting point: "Thus the title of the novel, *Mrs. Dalloway,* which emphasizes the social radiancy and centrality of its heroine, yields to and is absorbed by its transformative ending—'It is Clarissa, he said'—an ending that is both the meeting-point and the terminal point of Clarissa Dalloway's quest for social and spiritual integration."[16] At the beginning of the day, Clarissa is undiscriminating in her enjoyment of the flow of sensations, but she gradually manages to find a midpoint between this subjectivity and the abstraction of Bradshaw: "neither dependence nor rejection—that is the final synthesis of Mrs. Dalloway."[17] Considering the alternatives available to her, Clarissa has trodden a fine line between the masculine anger of Miss Kilman and the feminine surrender of Sally Seton. She has given up passion for privacy; she has compromised but has avoided becoming marginalized. She has stayed near the center of power in a position of influence, yet she also has a room of her own. Her day is threaded between "the melting away of the shell of the self by the sun's heat and the freezing of it again into a hard crust by the thetic winter of Big Ben."[18]

And yet, and yet . . . When Woolf decided not to have Clarissa commit suicide but to create a subplot in which that event might happen, was she simply finding a means for Clarissa to have it both ways? Or did she begin to articulate a cause-and-effect, dialectical relationship between different sections of society? Woolf did insist that the two characters were "entirely dependent upon each other,"[19] but to argue that Clarissa and Septimus are "the opposite sides of the same coin"[20] is to sentimentalize the novel and pull its critical teeth. To see the connection between Septimus and Clarissa as that of mother and son[21] is further to subvert their essential opposition.

We must not lose sight of the facts. When Clarissa hears of Septimus's death she is entertaining his murderer. The forces that restrained Clarissa from self-fulfillment in her youth are the same forces that caused both the war and Septimus's derangement. English society is rotten to the core with the suppression of emotion, and Clarissa is simply the most sophisticated example of a hierarchy of efficient thought police. No mystical yearning can justify the waste and oblivion of millions of young lives: "No ceremonial conclusion to the war could restore the continuities it had ended, or recreate those 'fictions' that had been left behind in the labyrinth of the trenches."[22] While Clarissa herself wishes for a symbolic absorption of Septimus, he actually remains a stubborn, unassimilable fact. Postwar English society does not integrate him but spits him out. This essentially tragic view of the novel is shared by many critics, such as Allen McLaurin, for whom Clarissa's party is "only a symbolic gesture, a greeting to other human beings across the emptiness which she sees at the heart of life."[23] Or, as Leaska puts it, "In Septimus's death, she becomes the spectator of her own tragedy."[24] Clarissa's compromises have been too many and too great. For one critic, "her life is not much more than vivacity . . . a grave insistence upon the dissipation and death of her spirit in glittering triviality."[25] Her plunge into life on the first page we recognize at the end as not dissimilar to Septimus's fatal plunge. Her whole life is one drawn-out suicide; thus, "It is the beauty and the fun of the life she has denied herself that Septimus's suicide calls up, not the life she must go back to."[26]

In this reading Septimus is not at all on the same level as Clarissa but is, rather, connected in a chain of cause and effect. When Clarissa threw her coin into the Serpentine she was demonstrating her wealth and position, as well as her optimism for the future. As Shakespeare's dirge goes on to say, she has "taken her wages" from Richard every day since her marriage. Septimus has no money. His only "treasure" is his life, and when he "flings" himself out the window, shouting, "I'll give it you!" he is talking not to Clarissa but to Holmes, the "serpent" who has disrupted his Eden that he shared momentarily with the birdlike Rezia, surrounded by dappled sunlight, flowers, and hats. In effect, Septimus is flinging Clarissa's filthy lucre back in her face, and Clarissa's response is ghoulishly to feed off his disaster.

The memories Woolf invented for Clarissa at Bourton do soften her character for us, and through Clarissa's nostalgia and regret we feel some of the sensitivity that animates Septimus's grief and guilt. But a resistance to Clarissa remains, as Woolf herself sensed when her friend Lytton Strachey commented on the character's ambiguity: "I think some distaste for her persisted. But again, that was true of my feeling for Kitty, and one must dislike people in art without its mattering."[27] As Suzanne Henke puts it, Clarissa shares both Greek and Christian qualities. She plays the role of empathic victim to the crucified Septimus, but also the role of high priestess of the party.[28] For Gilbert and Gubar, Clarissa is "a kind of queen," who "with a divine grace . . . regenerates the post-war world that has 'undone' Septimus, Phlebas, T. S. Eliot and all too many others."[29] But Clarissa is wedded to the system and knows that she has compromised to get there. Does her spiritual uncertainty really change anything? The mean, powerful men continue to rule. They impose their beat upon others, and those who do not march in step (like Lady Bradshaw or Septimus) can only opt out into marginalization or death. Possible saviours like Miss Kilman have their own problems and loneliness, and may desperately need to possess rather than to love.

We have come round to a condemnation of Clarissa Dalloway, but such an interpretation depends on a thorough understanding of Septimus's predicament as the result of specific social forces in post-war England. And when we consider the larger social scene, even Clarissa comes to seem more like a victim of a system she is powerless to change.

SEPTIMUS SMITH AND SHELL SHOCK

Septimus Smith

Under thirty years old, hawklike with a big nose, he was a "poet in Stroud" outside London before he came to the city and worked in Sibleys and Arrowsmiths, auctioneers and land agents. When war was declared he was one of the first to volunteer. His best friend, the officer Evans, was killed in Italy before the armistice in 1918. Septimus met and married Rezia while he was billeted in Milan. They now live off Tottenham Court Road.

Lucrezia Warren Smith

The younger daughter of a Milan innkeeper, she met and married Septimus at the end of the war. She now makes hats for her landlady, Mrs. Filmer, and for Mrs. Filmer's daughter, Mrs. Peters, who is expecting a baby.

Doctor William Bradshaw

The son of a shopkeeper, he has had thirty years' experience as a psychiatrist in Harley Street, London. He makes twelve thousand pounds a year and has a son doing well at Eton. His wife, Lady Bradshaw, "went under" fifteen years ago—that is, submerged her personality for the sake of her husband's career.

It was the poet Wilfred Owen who wrote the lines "Move him into the sun," expressing his despair at the waste of young men's lives. Woolf was familiar with the major writers of the Great War. She even bathed naked with Rupert Brooke,[30] but her term for him and his coterie—the "Neo-pagans"—is full of mockery. It was Siegfried Sassoon (his initials suspiciously like Septimus Smith's) whom Woolf most admired. She reviewed his work and he visited her in 1924. Her review of his poetry in May 1917 suggests that the struggling novelist may have learned from Sassoon's technique: "To call back any moment of emotion is to call back with it the strangest odds and ends that have become somehow part of it, and it is the weeds pulled up by mistake with the flowers that bring back the extraordinary moment as a whole."[31] In a second review, of Sassoon's *Counter-Attack and Other Poems* (July 1918), Woolf struggled to accommodate his brutal frankness. His sarcasm and horror were not poetry, but perhaps "beauty and art have something too universal about them to meet our particular case" and perhaps Sassoon was right to stick with "the raw stuff of poetry."[32]

Woolf was aware, then, of the difficulty involved in herself, a woman who had heard the guns of France only from a great distance, attempting to portray a war veteran like Septimus Smith. But by

Paul Nash, *Wytschaete Woods, 1917*. Reproduced by permission of the Manchester City Art Gallery/Rutherston Loan Collection.

choosing a victim of shell shock she was choosing someone whose mental experiences she had brushed against during her own bouts of mental illness. And her real focus was not so much his chaotic view of the world as society's view of him.

It is therefore important that we take some time to understand the full historical, sociological, and psychological details of this mental disorder that is Woolf's focus for both describing and criticizing her society.

The Victorian attitude toward abnormal behavior tended to be judgmental and usually required the sufferer to be shut off from society. As one historian puts it, "One characteristic of the mid-Victorian faith in institutions embodied in bricks and mortar, was a growing popular belief (which seems slowly to have worked its way up the social scale) that the best place for the insane was an asylum."[33] As Dr. Bradshaw explains it to Rezia, "[Septimus] had threatened to kill himself. There was no alternative. It was a question of law. He would lie in bed in a beautiful house in the country" (107).

From 1919, however, Sigmund Freud's ideas were slowly making their way into England. Indeed, as early as 1907 General Booth of the Salvation Army opened the first "Anti-Suicide Bureau" in London. Through the Hogarth Press, which eventually published Freud's complete works in English, Woolf was in the vanguard of this contact. A book of 1923 intended to popularize Freud's views explains the new role of psychologists as mediators rather than manipulators. Its author, J. H. van der Hoop, insists that "no serious psycho-analyst will force his treatment upon a patient"[34] and hopes that in the future "we shall come to realize that our conflicts about ideas and principles are often no more than disguised attempts to domineer and to suppress the opinions of others, who after all have as much right to their own ideas as we have. This point of view may shock those people who consider their own judgments to be the only right ones."[35]

The major challenge to British psychiatry in the 1920s was shell shock. The term *shell shock* was coined by C. S. Myers in 1915, and Showalter suggests that its popularity had to do with its manly sound, in contrast to the identical condition that had been known for decades under the name of *hysteria,* a word etymologically linked with the female reproductive organs.[36] British society was ill-prepared to acknowledge, let alone deal with, this mental disorder. Woolf saw in this unpreparedness a perfect metaphor for her critique of a society that demanded regimentation and denied sensitivity. What was shell shock? It was "a condition of alternate moods of apathy and high excitement, with very quick reaction to sudden emergencies but no capacity for concentrated thinking. . . . Its effects passed off very gradually. In most cases the blood was not running pure again for four or five years; and in numerous cases men who had managed to avoid a nervous breakdown during the war collapsed badly in 1921 or 1922."[37] The psychological basis of the war neuroses was "an elaboration with endless variations of one central theme: escape from an intolerable situation in real life to one made tolerable by neurosis."[38]

Sassoon's poetry vividly described shell shock. A poem of 1917 describing a crazed soldier, in grief because of his brother's death, sarcastically concludes with the officer's belief that "such men have lost all patriotic feeling."[39] Another poem of that year describes the "Survivors":

> No doubt they'll soon get well; the shock and strain
> Have caused their stammering, disconnected talk.
> Of course they're "longing to go out again,"
> These boys with old scared faces, learning to walk.
> They'll soon forget their haunted nights; their cowed
> Subjection to the ghosts of friends who died,—
> Their dreams that drip with murder; and they'll be proud
> Of glorious war that shatter'd all their pride . . .
> Men who went out to battle, grim and glad;
> Children, with eyes that hate you, broken and mad.[40]

Sassoon's own experience of battle and shell shock moved him to celebrate natural things like birds and leaves with an intensity that recalls both Septimus and Clarissa: "O beauty, born of lovely things that die!"[41] In Sassoon's novel-memoir *The Complete Memoirs of George Sherston* (1937), the hero could be the prewar Septimus, outside Clarissa's florist: "I had visions of Mayfair in June, and all the well-oiled ingredients of affluence and social smartness. . . . Sighing for such splendors, I knew that I was only flattening my nose against the plate-glass window of an expensive florist's shop."[42] But after the war, as George convalesces—again like Septimus, but with more understanding doctors—Sassoon observes:

> But by night each man was back in his doomed sector of a horror-stricken Front Line, where the panic and stampede of some ghastly experience was re-enacted among the livid faces of the dead. No doctor could save him then, when he became the lonely victim of his dream disasters and delusions.
>
> Shell-shock. How many a brief bombardment had its long-delayed after-effect in the minds of these survivors, many of whom had looked at their companions and laughed while inferno did its best to destroy them. Not then was their evil hour but now; now, in

the sweating suffocation of nightmare, in paralysis of limbs, in the stammering of dislocated speech.[43]

By the end of the war in 1918, 80,000 cases of shell shock had been treated by army doctors,[44] and during the decade 1919–29 there were 114,600 applications for pensions related to shell shock.[45] Pensions for psychotic illness actually increased after the war: the British government awarded more in 1929 than in the four years following the war.[46] From 1916 to 1920, 4 percent of British casualties were psychiatric, but by 1932, 36 percent of veterans receiving disability pensions were psychiatric casualties.[47] In other words, although the flood of neurasthenic war veterans needing treatment peaked at 100,000 in 1922, the repercussions of trench warfare were felt in England long after that. The psychologist Carl Jung observed this phenomenon when he dreamed in 1926 of being back in the trenches: "The happenings in the dream suggested that the war, which in the outer world had taken place some years before, was not yet over, but was continuing to be fought within the psyche."[48]

Initial reactions to shell shock by the military doctors were brutal, and Holmes and Bradshaw exemplify this brutality. One of the leading researchers into the phenomenon remembered hearing a fellow medical officer declare that if there was no evidence of organic damage to the central nervous system, the individual concerned should be shot.[49] The *War Office Committee of Inquiry into Shell-Shock* (1922) was, according to Zwerdling, "an extraordinary document. It shows very little sympathy for such victims of the war, insists that often 'shell-shock' is indistinguishable from cowardice or insubordination, and argues that these breakdowns are usually the product of a 'congenital or acquired pre-disposition to pathological reaction in the individual concerned.' The recommendations for treatment are a blend of persuasion and coercion."[50]

But as increasing numbers of sensible young men came back, like Septimus Smith, mentally shattered from the front, explanations like moral inferiority or cowardice no longer sufficed. Septimus's description of the war as "that little shindy of schoolboys with gunpowder"

(106) is a sarcastic reference to Bradshaw's inflexible views. Through shell shock the medical profession and the public at large were forced to reappraise their attitudes toward the mind. Woolf suggested this enforced reappraisal of the human mind when she wrote, in her biography of Roger Fry, that "a break must be made in every life when August 1914 is reached."[51] Military and private doctors began to draw on Freud's ideas about neurosis and the subconscious, and in this way the Freudians managed to secure a foothold in British psychiatry.[52] Freud himself wrote an introduction to a study of shell shock in 1919,[53] and concluded his findings in a letter to Ernest Jones: "The difference between peace and war is that with the former the ego is strong but surprised, with the latter it is prepared but weakened."[54] For the general public, to whom the terms *ego* and *libido* were still strange, the numbers of cases of shell shock in Britain's streets and hospitals nevertheless meant a heightened awareness to the "normality" of the abnormal: "it gradually became apparent that much of what had been considered abnormal might be discovered in the mind of the average man."[55]

Even "normal" returned soldiers suffered from memories of the war, and Woolf makes Septimus articulate and often (as in his last scene) calm in order to suggest that he is not an exception. Many soldiers felt guilty that they were alive at all. Richard Aldington's novel *Death of a Hero* (1929) articulates this point: "What right have I to live? Is it five million, is it ten million, is it twenty million? What does the exact count matter? There they are and we are responsible. Tortures of hell, we are responsible. . . . It is dreadful to have outlived your life, to have shirked your fate, to have overspent your welcome."[56] Robert Graves reported his reaction to the backfiring of a car in London after the war: instead of straightening his back like Clarissa, he dived into a ditch.[57]

As we read *Mrs. Dalloway* we tend to pair and contrast Peter and Septimus, because they are both suffering from loneliness and repression. Through them, Woolf suggests that madness and shell shock have profound implications for the power and management of the social group. The war itself depended on the individual's submission to the group and the nation. Specifically "sexual" impulses had no place on the battlefield. Ideas of male camaraderie, epitomized by Lord Kitchener's organization of "Pals" (at least, until 1917), fostered manliness and brotherhood, and many British doctors felt that shell shock had effectively disproved Freud's theory of sexuality. These doctors claimed that the illness resulted from a conflict between fear and duty in the soldier's mind. In his article on shell shock, however, Freud suggested that the repression of fear in war is analogous to the repression of the libido in peace; in both cases, the repression is for the sake of the group, to prevent its "disintegration." In their pioneering study of shell shock in 1917, Smith and Pear drew out the consequences of their study for peacetime: "The suppression of fear and other strong emotions is not demanded only of men in the trenches. It is constantly expected in ordinary society."[58] Freud supported this idea in his essay on group psychology, translated and published by the Hogarth Press in 1922: "A neurosis has the same disintegrating effect upon a group as being in love."[59] It has taken recent feminist historians and critics to make explicit the link between battle and sexual disruption. Sandra Gilbert, for example, observes that far from enhancing male sexual instincts "the war emasculated and confined men as closely as any Victorian woman."[60]

Despite these profound dislocations, English society after the war showed an amazing ability to deny or forget psychological, sexual, and social change. So Peter Walsh admires the young soldiers still marching through London's streets. Only those people who themselves were profoundly changed would continue to see life differently. Woolf noted of Septimus in her diary: "He must somehow see through human nature—see its hypocrisy, & insincerity, its power to recover from every wound, incapable of taking any final impression. His sense that this is not worth having."[61] That shameful awareness is shared by other characters such as Clarissa and Peter, so that while " 'deferred shell-shock' is Sir William Bradshaw's diagnosis of Septimus's malady . . . deferred war-shock might, perhaps, be our account of the total motif of *Mrs. Dalloway*."[62]

Septimus is one returned soldier who refuses to be treated as a herd animal, although he begins to see the rest of humanity as animalistic and doomed. Even his name suggests a uniqueness that puts him beyond the "Smiths" of this world. Mitchell Leaska argues that the character's curious first name derives from Dante's *Inferno,* which Septimus is reading: the seventh ("septimus") circle of Hell is where punishment is given to those who have been violent against others or themselves.[63] I have elsewhere suggested that Smith's Latinate name also recalls Shakespeare's *Cymbeline,* set in Britain and Italy, from which comes the refrain "Fear no more": "Like Posthumus, Septimus is a noble and slighted warrior. He is also an avid Shakespearean scholar."[64]

Leaska tries to universalize Septimus's predicament by stressing his homosexual love for Evans and by claiming that nowhere is his illness actually linked to shell shock. In fact, at the party Bradshaw talks to Richard Dalloway "about the deferred effects of shell shock" (202) in connection with the death of Septimus. The foregoing discussion of shell shock shows how the condition might lead to such peacetime neuroses as the suppression of the libido. This outcome is clearly true in Septimus's case. He has no sexual relations at all with his wife, even though she is young, energetic, and dreams of babies.

It is not difficult to generalize a picture of a sensitive young man (a poet) brutalized by the industrial world, whether in the trenches or in the factories. His sanctuary is "Miss Isabel Pole, lecturing in the Waterloo Road upon Shakespeare" (94). Filled with the image of Miss Pole and the imagery of Shakespeare, young Septimus went off to France and managed to maintain his sensitivity through a close relationship (not necessarily homosexual) with Evans, his officer. The strain on Septimus's psyche was extreme: as Freud described the process, Septimus learned to deny the urgings of his subconscious self toward simple self-preservation, while at the same time continuing "human" relationships. Now, in peacetime, the situation is reversed. Septimus regards his libido, or his self-concious sensitivity and sensuality, as disgusting and threatening. He therefore alternates between uncensored joy at the sensual pleasures of Regent's Park and hatred and loathing for existence and for his and all humanity.

Characters and Themes

Apart from trees (discussed earlier), there are two motifs Woolf uses to dramatize Septimus's predicament. One is dogs. Evans and he are described as "a case of two dogs playing on a hearth-rug . . . they had to be together, share with each other, fight with each other, quarrel with each other" (96). In peacetime, the image is monstrously inverted and puppy love becomes bestiality: a Skye terrier turns into a man before Septimus's eyes (76), while a man—the ghost of Evans—lurks "behind the railings" (28). Since the next page mentions the nearby Regent's Park Zoo, with its "dun-colored animals . . . barking, howling" (29), we can assume that Septimus is associating his former love with animals locked up in cages. Men have turned themselves into beasts through what William Blake would call the "mind-forg'd manacles" of mental abstractions like patriotism. The railings, of course, continue this image pattern into Septimus's last moments: when he flings himself down on the area railings he is, as it were, trying to break open the cage and free Evans, along with all humanity.

The second motif Woolf uses is language. Septimus has a poet's sensitivity to language and metaphor. The narrator suggests his opposite when she has Peter Walsh recall Richard Dalloway "getting on his hind legs" (84) to denounce the sonnets of Shakespeare. This animal image alludes to Dr. Johnson's infamous description of a woman speechifying: like a standing dog, the wonder is that she can do it at all. Septimus's love of Shakespeare was instinctual and earthy, and bound up with his love for Miss Pole. Now that he has seen utter physical degradation, Septimus has deconstructed Shakespeare. Now he feels that "love between man and woman was repulsive to Shakespeare. The business of copulation was filth to him before the end" (99). Nevertheless, Septimus still identifies Shakespeare's words with Nature's (155), and the novel itself secretly supports his preference: Clarissa quotes Shakespeare several times, while institutional characters like Bradshaw, Dalloway, and Lady Bruton do not care for Shakespeare.

Totally alienated from his society, Septimus, not surprisingly, feels robbed of the English language itself. This feeling may be a reason for his marrying a foreigner. He has not simply "deconstructed" the great texts; he has stumbled upon a universal *aporia* (a term used by deconstructive critics like Jacques Derrida to describe the way meaning opens up endlessly into other meanings and can never be pinned down): "This was now revealed to Septimus; the message hidden in the beauty of words. The secret signal which one generation passes, under disguise, to the next is loathing, hatred, despair. Dante the same. Aeschylus (translated) the same" (98). Now that the English language seems corrupted, Septimus tries to listen to the language of Nature itself. He hears the sparrows singing in Greek about how there is neither crime nor death (28); later the voice is Evans's as he sings among the orchids in Thessaly; and the tune of a beggar's penny whistle transcends space as well as time to sing, like Keats's nightingale, of beauty and truth (78). Woolf cleverly interweaves these stock Greek and romantic pastoral allusions with the modern poetry of T. S. Eliot. Septimus, whose great fear is that he cannot feel, is Eliot's hollow man who sees the city as already devastated in some holocaust. The only language he has access to, whether natural or literary, is ruined fragments.

The narrator constantly refers to this question of language and the dilemma of someone who is in need of a meaning framework but who has rejected the one framework available. "Septimus could take Dr Holmes's word for it—there was nothing whatever the matter with him," says the narrator (102). But that is precisely what Septimus resists: he will not "take" the language of power any longer. Marginalized, his only recourses are either to a universal language like that in the sky ("he could not read the language yet; but it was plain enough, this beauty, this exquisite beauty"[25]) or to the private language of his ravings, which Rezia writes down but which no one can understand. Septimus tries to connect with the society and nature about him because he "knew the meaning of the world" (74). He wants to communicate but his message is like the sign-writing plane's, meaningless *because* it tries to be in a non-Shakespearean Esperanto or universal language. In one of the numerous puns that appropriately litter those "wordy" passages dealing with Septimus, his words fall from his lips like "shavings from a plane" (78).

Being a foreigner, Rezia can more easily reject English society. Her tragedy is that the world she wants to join in order to begin a new life with her husband is precisely the one from which he would flee. Rezia is compromised by the language and attitudes she is struggling to learn. Near the beginning of the novel she calls Septimus a "coward" (27) for wanting to die, and this, ironically, is exactly what Holmes calls him when he plunges. But Rezia is also a shrewd judge of character and learns quickly. She decides that Bradshaw is not "a nice man" and tries to keep Holmes away from her husband. The last we see of her, she is lying on a couch while the dark bulk of Holmes looms over her, blocking out the sun and suggestive of a lecherous rapist who has broken in and destroyed their "home." Holmes is indeed Septimus's image of "human nature . . . the repulsive brute, with the blood-red nostrils. Holmes was on him" (102). Now the succubus has swapped one victim for another.

Rezia's pathetic impotence is underlined by ironic parallels between her and Clarissa, the other wife. Rezia works at making hats. These fashionable fripperies which Clarissa would buy in Bond Street for one wearing are for Rezia an economic livelihood and a form of art. Both women are artists: just as Clarissa creates elegant beauty in her party, so Rezia creates affordable beauty in her hats. But there the similarity ends. Unlike Clarissa, Rezia spends her day at her husband's side, but he keeps leaving her in his mind; Richard keeps coming back to Clarissa like a faithful dog. Rezia is lonely, bewildered, and helpless in an alien land. The ironic parallels between the two women culminate in Rezia's reaction to her husband's suicide. Echoing Clarissa's actions on the opening page, Rezia is "opening long windows, stepping out into some garden" (166), but we know that her vision has been drug-induced by Holmes and that she faces an uncertain future.

Although the Smiths are losers, they embody much of the energy and delight in *Mrs. Dalloway.* Despite the crazed, disjointed rhetoric leading up to Septimus's final scene, Woolf shows us Septimus and Rezia sharing their best moment of sheer joy and exhilaration just before Holmes intrudes. Woolf wins our sympathy for both the Smiths in this peaceful scene with its childlike charm. It is Holmes who seems aggressive, even pathological; Septimus as he prepares for death is totally rational, totally ordinary. He will not use the bread knife, because he doesn't want to spoil it. He acknowledges that what he is about to do will be the doctors' "idea of tragedy" (165) although it is not his. In fact Septimus "did not want to die" (165).

Septimus's simple declaration stays in the reader's mind like an incontrovertible accusation against Clarissa's society. When Clarissa rewrites the death scene in her mind at the end of the novel, we cannot forget his love of life. Clarissa insulates herself against his challenge by turning him into a work of art, an exemplary tale that "made her feel the beauty, made her feel the fun." But he refuses to be reduced to a symbol or to become an actor in someone else's tragedy. The reader cannot forget Septimus's earlier protest that "the whole world was clamoring: Kill yourself, kill yourself, for our sakes. But why should he kill himself for their sakes?" (102–3).

Richard Dalloway and His Kind

Richard Dalloway

> A member of Parliament in the Conservative government, he looks forward to writing a history of the Bruton family when the Conservatives are voted out, which will be quite soon. He is "grey, dogged, dapper, clean" and has fair hair and blue eyes. He is a sportsman who cares for dogs.

Hugh Whitbread

> Variously described as being fifty-one or fifty-five, he has "a little job at Court." His family comprised coal merchants, but he admires royalty and English tradition. He writes letters to the Times about protecting owls in Norfolk and improving public shelters. Peter Walsh calls him "a toady." Hugh has known Lady Bruton for twenty years. His wife ("the Honorable Evelyn") is ill and has come up to London from the country to stay at a nursing home.

Lady Millicent Bruton

> *Sixty-two years old, granddaughter of General Sir Talbot Moore. Her family home is at Aldmixton in Devon, but she lives in London, on Brook Street. Her companions are Milly Brush (age forty) and her dog, a chow; her pastime is advocating for the emigration of poor English families to Canada. Lady Bruton reminds Peter Walsh of the eighteenth century.*

Woolf's "Mrs. Brown" lived, inevitably, in London. It was the city Woolf grew up in, knew well, and loved. In *A Room of One's Own* she writes, "London was like a workshop. London was like a machine. We were all being shot backwards and forwards on this plain foundation to make some pattern."[65] A series of pieces written for *Good Housekeeping* in 1931–32 demonstrate Woolf's intimate knowledge of London's highways, byways, and waterways. She discriminates between Bond Street, which Clarissa makes for at the opening of *Mrs. Dalloway* and where fashion "withdraws discreetly to perform its more sublime rites,"[66] and Oxford Street, with its "glassiness, its transparency." She struggles to appreciate the new architecture, with its philosophy of "built to pass, not to last." She senses the battles that have gone within "Great Men's Houses," such as the house of Thomas Carlyle. Everywhere in London, inside and out, there is life and conflict, except in a few secluded parks and graveyards: "The only peaceful places in the whole city are perhaps these old graveyards which have become gardens and playgrounds. . . . Here one might drowse away the first days of spring or the last days of autumn without feeling too keenly the stir of youth or the sadness of old age."[67] In such a mood Peter makes for Regent's Park, and Septimus searches fruitlessly for solace there.

Visiting the House of Commons, the haunt of Richard Dalloway, Woolf notices that individuality has given way to committees: "matters of great moment, which affect the happiness of people, the destinies of nations, are here at work chiselling and carving these very ordinary human beings." This is democracy, she admits, but her "corrupt mind"

Aerial view of Westminster Abbey and the Houses of Parliament.

hankers after the good old days when there were great men and characters in London, the kind of people Clarissa would love to have at her
party: "The mind, it seems, likes to perch, in its flight through empty
space, upon some remarkable nose, some trembling hand; it loves the
flashing eye, the arched brow, the abnormal, the particular, the splendid
human being."[68]

London satisfied Woolf because there she could reconcile the contraries of public and private life, rub shoulders with aristocrats and
commoners, feel a part of British history, but also withdraw indoors to
the privacy of her room or the intimate friendship of her Bloomsbury
group. As we saw in an earlier chapter, after the war the disparity
between nation and individual was more marked to her, and more in
opposition. She could not maintain her Victorian love of national
unity while championing subjective reality. In 1918 she lamented the

passing of a time of united purpose, and social life seemed trivial to her: "One feels now that the whole bunch has burst asunder & flown off with the utmost vigor in different directions. We are once more a nation of individuals. . . . One's sense of perspective is so changed that one cannot see at first what meaning all this gossip of parties can possibly have; one can't be interested."[69]

By 1923 she had sorted out her allegiances. The "gossip of parties" mattered, but not at the expense of the common people. She had seen the uniformed casualties of patriotism walking in the streets of her beloved London. Her attention had turned to the dispossessed and the alienated, the Septimus Smiths and Doris Kilmans of the metropolis. The cracks appearing in British social life revealed to her the depths of human depravity and its thin veneer of civility.

Richard Dalloway belongs, dinosaurlike, to a passing race of favored men who thrived in this veneer. The political world of Richard and Hugh Whitbread was narrowly chauvinistic, being self-selected by class as well as by sex, because at this time "the House of Commons represented a predominantly middle- and upper-class complexion. No less than 68 per cent of Conservative MPs of the period 1920–40 had been educated at public schools, over a quarter, 27.5 per cent, at Eton. . . . If the political rulers of Britain were drawn predominantly from the upper and middle classes, the senior elements in the Civil Service were even more socially exclusive."[70] By the 1920s, when Woolf was writing *Mrs. Dalloway,* Britain was looking for new leaders. As Zwerdling points out, "the Conservative Prime Minister who appears at Clarissa's party at the end of the book remained in office only until January 1924, when he was succeeded by the first Labour Prime Minister, Ramsay MacDonald. . . . As a class and as a force, then, the world to which the Dalloways belong is decadent rather than crescent."[71]

As early as the 1910s, and more especially after the war, Woolf was coming to terms with the kind of grand Victorian paterfamilias epitomized by her own father, Sir Leslie Stephen, and by those men he spent much of his life annotating in the *Dictionary of National Biography,* of which he was editor. We can see the outcome of this reeducation in

Woolf's diary comments about her cousin, Harry Stephen, who was once a judge of the high court in Calcutta, and was now an alderman on the London County Council. In 1918 Woolf observed his habit, which she bequeathed to Peter Walsh: "He still takes out an enormous pocket knife, & slowly half opens the blade, & shuts it."[72] A few months later she noted, "He has need of the Royal Family. . . . The impenetrable wall of the middle class conservative was never more stolid."[73] Woolf came to a vivid awareness of the power of these men as she followed the conduct of the war. One can sense her horrified realization, in October 1918, that a family friend, Herbert Fisher, had come to visit straight from the prime minister's residence on Downing Street: "the fate of armies does more or less hang upon what two or three elderly gentlemen decide."[74] Later, in her "Sketch of the Past," she described the "patriarchal machinery" of her family with scorn: "Every one of our male relations was shot into that machine and came out the other end, at the age of sixty or so, a Headmaster, an Admiral, a Cabinet Minister, a Judge. It is as impossible to think of them as natural human beings as it is to think of a plough horse galloping wild and unshod in the street."[75]

We can see how Woolf's attitude toward men in power changed and matured, by comparing the Richard Dalloway of *Mrs. Dalloway* with the Richard Dalloway of *The Voyage Out*. In her first novel, Woolf introduced the Dalloways for a short but memorable cameo appearance on board a yacht. Dalloway is described as "a gentleman who thinks that because he was once a member of Parliament, and his wife's the daughter of a peer, they can have what they like for the asking."[76] He declares,

> "May I be in my grave before a woman has the right to vote in England! That's all I say."
> The solemnity of her husband's assertion made Clarissa grave.
> "It's unthinkable," she said. (44)

To the young heroine Rachel Vinrace, Richard embodies all the power of imperial England. He "seemed to come from the humming oily center of the machine where the polished rods are sliding, and the pistons thumping" (48). Shortly after this mechanical metaphor, the British Mediterranean fleet is sighted and Richard murmurs in awe, "It's the continuity" (53). In the person of Rachel, Woolf pursues her interrogation of her father's generation. Rachel asks Richard what is his ideal, and he answers, "Unity of aim, of dominion, of progress" (69). Rachel wants to learn about this mysterious male world from him, but "Richard never met, never wants to meet a woman who understands 'statesmanship' " (72). In his view, women should remain domestic, with their illusions undisturbed.

As if Dalloway's male chauvinism isn't damning enough, Woolf reveals him to be a lecherous hypocrite as well. The only glimpse we have of Richard's emotions is when he impulsively kisses Rachel then tears himself away. In modern terms, this action virtually amounts to a case of child abuse (it recalls Woolf's own mistreatment at the hands of her half-brother George Duckworth).[77] The incident is replayed in *Mrs. Dalloway* between Sally Seton and Hugh Whitbread at Bourton. In fact Hugh Whitbread is at times a sarcastic summation of all the hypocritical men Woolf had known. Woolf's critique is clear and un-equivocal: Dalloway's machine morality has left him frustrated and incomplete, his concept of sexuality reduced to power play. He is able to walk away from his assault, but poor Rachel keeps it to herself. Its furtiveness and Dalloway's immunity contribute to sending her into a feverish madness and eventual death.

Another key scene of *Mrs. Dalloway* also had its origins in *The Voyage Out*. Rachel asks Richard to imagine an elderly widow in her room in the suburbs of Leeds. Dalloway argues that the individual must be seen as part of the whole. Rachel protests that he has left out the old woman's emotions (71–72). This old woman resurfaces as Mrs. Brown in Woolf's essay, and then as the old woman across from Clarissa's window. She is a test for Clarissa, who must see her as an individual rather than as a statistic.

In *Mrs. Dalloway* Richard is given some sympathetic traits, espe-cially in his return to Clarissa with flowers after lunch. He genuinely needs her opposite qualities, refueling like a car from the pump of her emotions. Woolf described this process in *A Room of One's Own:* "He would open the door of [the] drawing-room or nursery, I thought, and find her among her children perhaps, or with a piece of embroidery on her knee—at any rate, the center of some different order and system of life, and the contrast between this world and his own, which might be the law courts or the House of Commons, would at once refresh and invigorate; and there would follow, even in the simplest talk, such a natural difference of opinion that the dried ideas in him would be fertilized anew."[78]

Several of Richard's worst faults are transferred to Whitbread and Bradshaw. Through Peter, Woolf mercilessly condemns the former: "Villains there must be, and, God knows, the rascals who get hanged for battering the brains of a girl out in a train do less harm on the whole than Hugh Whitbread and his kindness!" (191–92). Woolf's condemnation of Bradshaw in her essay on conversion is no less complete. Nevertheless, several contemporary English critics are angry that Woolf does not wholeheartedly condemn the Dalloway system. Terry Eagleton is disappointed that the only likely candidate for iconoclast, Peter Walsh, is himself compromised: thus "Mrs. Dalloway is protected by the novel from the full force of the damaging charges which might be listed against her."[79] Although Woolf's Bloomsbury group background separated her from the militaristic philistinism of Dalloway, Eagleton argues, she could not completely destroy the system of which she was a part because "the ethic of aesthetic individualism is a privileged one, dependent on a settled structure of wealth and leisure to protect it from the exigencies of work, hardship, responsibility, conformism. In this sense, the liberal scepticism of Woolf's emancipated aesthetes is not entirely unconstrained: it stops short, necessarily, at a radical questioning of the social structure on which, as a philosophy, it is parasitic. . . . The values of Woolf's novels, then, are at one point deviations from established upper-class life, at another point reflections of it."[80]

Similarly, Jeremy Hawthorn concludes his study of the novel: "Whilst being objective enough to be able to see what Clarissa lacks in her life, Virginia Woolf herself lacks the sort of experience and knowl-

edge which would allow her to present solutions to Clarissa's problems more convincing and lasting than that of a party. . . . It is her
inability to synthesize personality and act that prevents her exploring
it beyond a certain point, the inability of a social class that sees its
personalities to be separate from the acts of those who produce the
wealth they live on."[81] This is an acute criticism, because for all their
love of connection and the English nation, neither Richard nor Clarissa articulates that the Dalloways' wealth depends on the labor and
sacrifice of people like Septimus, Rezia, and the old woman opposite.
But Hawthorn goes further. He is dismayed not only because Woolf's
critique isn't total but because she doesn't give us a happy ending as
well: "We are given in the novel an extraordinarily powerful picture of
men and women fighting a central inadequacy in their lives—the inadequacy of alienation—but we are shown no real way of escape from
it."[82] I do not think that novels must always give us social programs.
Besides, through Septimus and his wars Richard and his kind *are*
unequivocally condemned for their ignorance or disregard of the common people. The "Great War" was an invention of Richard Dalloway's political detachment and his attachment to capitalism. By
promising and then shattering the men's hopes for genuine camaraderie and challenge, the war exposed capitalism's manipulative, inhuman face: "the life of the worker was the model for the soldier in an
industrialized war."[83] For example, the Welsh miners under Robert
Graves's command found that digging trenches was simply a continuation of peacetime work. The soldiers found themselves in a labyrinth
of trenches that literally denied anyone a perspective on the whole:
they were in the dark, cogs in a machine. They would not accept such
powerlessness again, and Septimus's death is just the beginning of that
social revolution.

Woolf also indicates that the fallout from the war is beginning to
destroy the system that created it in more subtle ways, by breaking
down the myths of home and the subservience of women on which
industrial society depended. Woolf's "Lady Bessborough" (in *A Room
of One's Own*) wrote in an earlier age that "no woman has any
business to meddle with [politics] or any other serious business,"[84] and

her avatars in *Mrs. Dalloway*, Lady Bexborough and Lady Bruton, accept the war and their own marginalization (Lady Bruton's emigration plan is simply a desperate attempt to export the problem). But the prewar suffragette movement gained irreversible momentum through women's wartime service: "Women, as well as men, experienced with the onset of war the collapse of those established, traditional distinctions between an "economic" world of business and a private world of sentiment. This felt collapse permitted a range of personal contacts that had been impossible in their former social lives where hierarchies of status ruled."[85]

Septimus, Rezia, Miss Kilman, and Elizabeth reflect these changes (see the next section), and Clarissa's tense aloofness as party hostess indicates the strain of maintaining the old ways. During the day she is forced to come into contact with maids, shop girls, workmen, Miss Kilman, the old woman opposite, and finally Septimus. Out of this "collapse" of social barriers might come the new order. In these ways, then, *Mrs. Dalloway* does meet Eagleton's and Hawthorn's demands for a new vision through a "radical questioning of the social structure."

ELIZABETH DALLOWAY AND FEMINISM

Elizabeth Dalloway

Seventeen years old, the only child of Richard and Clarissa. She is devoted to her dog, Grizzle; appears dark, almost Oriental; and is being tutored by Miss Kilman.

Miss Kilman

Over forty years old. Descended from an eighteenth-century German family (Kiehlman), she has a degree in modern history and teaches extension classes. During the war she was dismissed from her position teaching history at a school because of anti-German prejudice, despite the fact that her brother was killed in the war. Two years and three months ago, she was "born again" into Christianity. She has a high forehead and wears a green mackintosh because she believes no clothes suit her. "I'm plain, I'm unhappy," she confesses. She dotes on Elizabeth and dislikes Clarissa.

Women had slightly outnumbered men in England even before the war killed off one eligible man in every seven and seriously injured another, so that the problem of the "surplus woman" was much debated in postwar England. Women assistants continued to be employed in shops and offices to a far greater extent than before the war,[86] and opportunities for careers generally opened up. In 1919 Viscountess Astor became the first woman member of Parliament. Times had changed since the 1890s, when Sally Seton was accosted in the smoking room at Bourton by Hugh Whitbread, who kissed her on the lips "to punish her for saying that women should have votes" (201). Nevertheless, it was still an extremely sexist society by today's standards. Even Mrs. Baldwin, the prime minister's wife, declared that politics was "essentially a man's institution evolved through centuries by men to deal with men's affairs in a man's way."[87]

Progress was made during the 1920s, and it may be no coincidence that Woolf chose to set her novel in the year 1923, a time when the hard-won victories of the suffragettes and women war workers were slowly being translated into law and affecting social attitudes. In 1925, six important laws were passed concerning the rights of women: Guardianship of Infants; Widows' Pensions; Summary Jurisdiction; Adoption of Children; Midwives and Maternity Homes; and Criminal Justice. This last law removed a man's responsibility for his wife's actions by allowing that if a woman committed a crime in her husband's presence, she could be held liable. Freud and British sexologists were talking freely about sex, and in 1925 Dora Russell (second wife of Bertrand Russell) published *Hypatia*, which advocated frank indulgence in sexuality for men and women.

Recent feminists have suggested, however, that these apparent advances were actually regressions, enshrining heterosexual sex and the orgasm at the cost of such unconventional life-styles as lesbianism or celibacy.[88] Ironically, in *Mrs. Dalloway* only Septimus shares Dora Russell's optimism that men and their institutions can change and become more feminine, holistic, and nurturing. Miss Kilman is more cynical, and her distrust of men is shared by such contemporary feminists as Dale Spender. Women were still at risk from men and male inventions. Graves records that around 1922 "a woman in Mecklenburgh Square committed suicide when under psycho-analytic treatment,"[89] and Woolf in 1925 witnessed a woman pinned against railings by a car and crushed to death. She commented, "A great sense of the brutality and wildness of the world remains with me."[90]

The sense of the oppression of women in *Mrs. Dalloway* is most subtly symbolized by the ability or inability to inscribe or to write. As DiBattista observes, "Women do not write in *Mrs. Dalloway*."[91] Clarissa "never wrote a letter" to Peter; when she does, it is a polite card saying, "How heavenly it was to see him." When men write they move the world: Bradshaw writes with his pencil on his pink card; General Sir Talbot Moore writes a telegram ordering the troops to advance; Lady Bexborough holds in her hand a telegram from a military man telling of her son's death; even Lady Bruton needs Hugh to proofread her letter because he "was able to put things as editors liked them put" (121). Women do write occasionally—Sally writes letters to Peter but tears them up, Rezia records Septimus's pronouncements, and Miss Kilman presumably writes in her classes—but the point is that men have the power in words, as long as they support the system. Those men who opt out, such as Septimus, are reduced to scribbling on the backs of envelopes, disenfranchised like women from the communication game.

One of Woolf's subversive points in the novel is that the most influential communication is nonverbal. The most intimate communication between Rezia and Septimus occurs when they design a hat, using thread and flowers rather than pencil and paper. Similarly, Clarissa and Richard's most intimate exchange involves the gift of flowers. But in the real world the powerful (men) control all the signs, from the right gloves bought from the right shop, to the ministerial car. Only the unreadable sign in the sky remains enigmatic, like an oracle of a possible future in which every individual's interpretation is valued.

Miss Kilman is fighting men at their own game and is to an extent admired. Through Elizabeth, Clarissa feels a bond with her, almost a love. But Clarissa also sees Miss Kilman as a vampire (she reminds us of the goddess Conversion) because she has been possessed by theory; she has, in Woolf's wicked pun, "turned into a church" (137). Try as she may to be an extremist and despite her name, Miss Kilman is a civilized woman, and it is her failure as a social being that Clarissa criticizes. She has let herself be taken over by religion and wears a green mackintosh rather than caring for her appearance. Because we get to know Clarissa so intimately, we see that Miss Kilman is mistaken in her judgment that Clarissa is one of those who have "known neither sorrow nor pleasure; who have trifled [their] life away!" (138). On the contrary, Clarissa has felt, and still feels, the gamut of human emotions. Indeed she feels both love and hatred toward Miss Kilman: "Ah, how she hated her—hot, hypocritical, corrupt; with all that power; Elizabeth's seducer. . . . She hated her: she loved her" (193). The word *seducer* suggests that Clarissa sees her own history replaying itself in her daughter's lesbian attachment, which accounts for Clarissa's ambivalent attitude toward the relationship. No, Clarissa is alive and feeling; it is Miss Kilman who is denying her total being by trying to "rid herself both of hatred and of love" (148).

Woolf is also harsh on Lady Bruton, another woman who is apparently liberated. Instead of elevating her into a shining example of how women can wield power, Woolf exposes her as a dangerous, interfering "she-male," more jingoistic even than the admirable Hugh. In the following sentence Woolf seduces the reader with the first phrase, only to mock facile feminist answers with the second: "Debarred by her sex, and some truancy, too, of the logical faculty" (199). Lady Bruton has been co-opted into the male system, and there is little to separate her from Lady Bradshaw the performing seal, the "typical successful man's wife" (201).

Lady Bruton and Miss Kilman "are women infected with masculinity."[92] To Clarissa—and, one feels, to Woolf herself—they have sacrificed too much of their femininity in order to play in a man's world. Miss Kilman's religion and Lady Bruton's mania for emigration are both mono-myths that swamp the individual. Neither woman would have time for Septimus—not because he is a man but because he claims individuality. The suppression of individual expression, as Woolf glimpsed in 1913 in the Burley nursing home, is what the soul will not tolerate, even in women. The French feminist Julia Kristeva has warned against fanatical feminism in similar terms: "No-one is safe from totalitarianism, and women no more so than men; most recently we have seen how it can lead to sectarian female groups."[93]

What of the future? As she was to do with Cam Ramsay in her next novel, *To the Lighthouse,* Woolf resisted the easy solution of offering the next generation of women as saviours. Both Mrs. Dalloway's and Mrs. Ramsay's daughters are ambiguous about liberation. Elizabeth may decide on a professional career but might equally well become a hostess like her mother. She rebels against Clarissa and flirts with Miss Kilman's theories but does not challenge the binary terms and evaluations offered by the male system. It is hard to see her "seeking to modify its hierarchy or its terms of exclusion"[94] when all she wants is to be back in the country with her father and her dogs.

In fact, Woolf uses Elizabeth as a contrast to reinforce Clarissa's own considerable emancipation. Elizabeth is a gauche country girl. Compared with Clarissa's enthusiasm on the first page, her daughter's thoughts when she leaves the Army and Navy Stores—"It was so nice to be out of doors" (149)—seem bland. Indeed, Woolf goes on, Elizabeth "had no preferences. . . . She inclined to be passive." Although she explores up the Strand where no Dalloway has gone before, and does so like a swashbuckling pirate, there is implied criticism: she shoves people aside in her impetuosity to board the bus, and her vague ideas of a profession evaporate as "silliness." Like Peter and Clarissa, Elizabeth abandons discrimination in a vague fellow feeling inspired by the military music. Should we go along with the mass, or try to challenge authority and change things that need to be changed? We can stay on the surface, enjoying with Elizabeth Dalloway the martial music in Fleet Street because "it was not conscious. There was no recognition in it of one's fortune, or fate, and for that very reason even to those dazed with watching for the last shivers of consciousness on the faces of the dying, consoling" (153). The novel as a whole articulates and celebrates "this voice . . . this vow; this van; this life; this procession" (153). Elizabeth's moment in Fleet Street is a prelude to her mother's moment at the party when Clarissa receives the news of another person's lonely death. The procession and the party go on, helping both mother and daughter to accept death. But for all Elizabeth's easy ecstasy, the woman behind that window above Fleet Street mourning is the individual Rezia, and her dead husband is the shell-shocked soldier Septimus. To her the martial music must sound like a grotesque mockery. Woolf's social world of national comradeship conceals dislocation and brutality.

When Woolf describes the examples of Elizabeth's female ancestors, the reader can sense the deflation of expectation, sentence by sentence, as she appropriates and then abandons the male imagery. As in the passage describing Lady Bruton, Woolf deliberately draws in the reader who is looking for saviours: "Abbesses, principals, head mistresses, dignitaries, in the republic of women—without being brilliant, any of them, they were that. She penetrated a little farther in the direction of St Paul's. She liked the geniality, sisterhood, motherhood, brotherhood of this uproar" (152). Elizabeth "penetrates" and enjoys "*brother*hood" (emphasis added): she valorizes these male ideas and accepts that the centers of male power, such as Fleet Street, the Strand, Lincoln's Inn, and St. Paul's, will remain male preserves. It is to Elizabeth that Woolf speaks in *A Room of One's Own:* "May I remind you that most of the professions have been open to you for close on ten years now?"[95]

Elizabeth's "adventure" ends with a remarkably supple passage describing how the clouds look both monumental and ephemeral. Unfortunately, the observation, with all its flexibility and irony, is Septimus's, not Elizabeth's. We leave her "calmly and competently" negotiating the steps of the bus and glimpse her only once more at the party, ill at ease, enjoying her father's praise but yearning to be in the country with her dog. Like the awful Lord Gayton and Miss Blow, Elizabeth lacks what the older generation has: the gifts of language and discursive thought. She is not even aware enough of her society to be uneasy.

With so few exemplary women, then, whence comes the novel's revolutionary force that has attracted so many feminist critics? It comes from the way the text itself represses, subverts, and challenges itself. Elizabeth Abel sees in the text a characteristic subterfuge whereby "an iconoclastic plot weaves its course covertly through the narrative grid."[96] The iconoclastic plot is the story of Septimus and Rezia that undermines the overt Clarissa plot; the questioning of society and the place of women in that society undermines its apparent endorsement.

That questioning has its origins deep in Clarissa's past, symbolized in the novel by what happened at Bourton. Abel suggests that Clarissa's world is hopelessly split, temporally and geographically, between Bourton and London, between a pastoral female world and a male sociopolitical one.[97] Bourton is suppressed in Clarissa's life just as the stories of the female characters are suppressed in the novel. The death of Clarissa's sister, Sylvia, for example, must have been a traumatic event, but it is reduced to one line. What is more, Clarissa's father seems to be to blame. (His name, Justin Parry, suggests justice as well as warfare, both male preserves.)

Clarissa is fully aware that her own greatest sexual experience occurred at Bourton, not with one of the courting young men but with Sally Seton. When Clarissa retreats nunlike to her room at noon to read the memoirs of a Napoleonic general, she recalls what might have been, had she not been physically frigid. Sexual pleasure is what she describes when she feels she lacks "something central which permeated; something warm which broke up surfaces and rippled the cold contact of man and woman, or of women together" (36). The phrase "women together" is the cue for her to recall her relationship with Sally, her feeling of "ecstasy" that young Clarissa at first tries to modify into a disinterested, chivalric feeling, possible only "between women just grown up" who are both anticipating the "catastrophe" of marriage. But this barely articulated feeling of shared victimization is soon replaced by Clarissa's moment (what Joyce would have called her epiphany) in the garden with Sally, "the most exquisite moment of her whole life. . . . Sally stopped; picked a flower; kissed her on the lips"

(40). We have already, as readers, divined the sexual nature of Clarissa's memory:

> It was a sudden revelation, a tinge like a blush which one tried to check and then, as it spread, one yielded to its expansion, and rushed to the farthest verge and there quivered and felt the world come closer, swollen with some astonishing significance, some pressure of rapture, which split its thin skin and gushed and poured with an extraordinary alleviation over the cracks and sores. Then, for that moment, she had seen an illumination; a match burning in a crocus; an inner meaning almost expressed. But the close withdrew; the hard softened. It was over—the moment. (36)

This amazing description of sexual orgasm works in terms of opposites: the female fleeing, the world approaching; the world gushing, the female "crack" bathed; the inner almost ex-pressed, pressed outward to meet the swollen world; the close far, the hard soft. It is an orchestration and resolution of opposites, marvelous but fleeting (Woolf was to use the same concatenation of images in her next novel, when the painter Lily Briscoe understands that life consists of daily illuminations, "matches struck unexpectedly in the dark").

Clarissa has forsaken such moments for her single bed and has turned her "catastrophe" of a marriage into a workable arrangement of convenience. She has left not only the company of women but also the company of men. Robbed by the male (Peter) of her one love, Sally, Clarissa in turn denies Peter by attaching herself to her daughter. Abel contrives to put Clarissa's moment in the little room in as positive a light as possible; Septimus's death "enables Clarissa to confront her loss"[98] (the passage describing her reaction to it parallels exactly the passage describing Clarissa's happiness with Sally), for "by recalling to Clarissa the power of her past and the only method of externalizing it, [Septimus] enables her fully to acknowledge and renounce its hold, to embrace the imperfect pleasures of adulthood more completely."[99] But such a reading blurs the enormity of Clarissa's sacrifice. The imagery of embracing is perhaps significantly chosen. In an earlier version of the scene, Rachel Bowlby points out, Clarissa went off "to breast her enemy" in a posture that suggests not a loving embrace but the aggression of Britannia.[100]

Abel's predicament is typical of critics who, while seeing the deficiencies in Clarissa, cannot help responding to the energy and warmth with which Woolf invests her. Although Clarissa's solution to her early disappointments may seem draconian and even desperate, we might be able to find ways in which her life as hostess may be a triumph of the female rather than a failure. After all, her success is to be measured in terms of her capacity to feel, rather than her capacity to dominate or hate men. Clarissa is still on the side of feeling, but she wants to embrace inclusively ("life"), not exclusively (Sally). She is mindful of the lesson of Shelley, whom she and Sally (her name an echo of the poet) read at Bourton, that the "longest journey" should not be made with one partner only. If she cannot have a woman for a lover, Clarissa will not have a man, either. Instead, she chooses society.

Some feminists see this self-denial as a tragic loss. But to examine the theoretical justifications for such a withdrawal we must look at the three strangest passages in the novel, passages in which Woolf was obviously pushed to break the flow of the text and debate this central issue of the place of sexuality, or the personal, in civilization.

The first passage is the "solitary traveler" section, Peter Walsh's reverie in the park. For Julia Carlson, the nameless woman is versions of Clarissa as Peter meets her at various times that day.[101] This view is to weaken the general truth, for the passage has to do with men's conception of women generally. Peter begins by imagining "the grey nurse" and metamorphoses her into a sequence of archetypal images of woman: spectral presence in the woods (a nymph); forgiving goddess dispensing absolution (the Virgin Mary?); wild carouser (the maenads?); harvest queen (Ceres?); siren or mermaid (63–64). Woolf shows how these images get in the way of the solitary male traveler's perception of "the actual thing." In frustration Peter eventually wishes to abandon his daily life and surrender himself to the great mother-goddess in the sky, who will "mount me on her streamers and let me blow to nothingness with the rest" (65). The words *mount* and *blow* are ambiguous. The first suggests both a mother putting a child onto a horse and a woman taking the dominant sexual position over a man. The second suggests the exhilarating freedom of the wind's abandonment but also the explosion of a bomb. The reader makes a connection between the male urge to oblivion in a lover's or a mother's arms and the alacrity with which so many young men rode or marched to their deaths in the war, a communal apocalypse with "the rest." In both cases, men act as children rather than as adults, seeking a "final solution" to their problems by confusing sex with death. In the words of Annie Leclerc,

> If man defines himself as "being-for-death," it is because, in the end, he derives his ultimate "definition," not from desire, which terminates nothing but only opens up new spaces, but from his pleasure, from the pleasure that puts an end to his desire.
>
> All they know is pleasure, which they call a "little death." They know of death only the horror of their pleasure, this incontestable pleasure where possession of the desired object escapes them just when it would seem to be within reach, this irrepressible pleasure, the assassin of their virility. The man who takes his pleasure is a man in the throes of death.[102]

Gilbert and Gubar make the same point not in the current language of feminist theory but through a revealing piece of historical evidence, a 1918 Red Cross War Relief poster called "The Greatest Mother in the World." In the position of the pietà an oversized nurse cradles a tiny bandaged soldier on his stretcher.[103]

There are two other women who wait on the traveler, but they are hardly more life affirming: the mother "whose sons have been killed in the battles of the world" (65) and Mrs. Turner, the landlady, clearing away the things. What do these three types offer to the solitary traveler? Orgasmic oblivion, mothering, and physical care. The solitary traveler sees woman in only these guises, as temptress, mother, or maid. He refuses to see women as individuals, like himself. Even Mrs. Turner, the most human, is barred from conversation by the male invention of class. Is it no wonder that at the end of his pilgrimage he is left alone at the table with no one to talk to?

The second irruption of the female into the narrative links Peter to the Smiths. The old woman at the Regent's Park Underground station sings her garbled song of love, apparently a lament for the beloved who was a victim of "death's enormous sickle" (90) and a reminder of the singer's own approaching death. Yet Woolf portrays the song as a fountain of life: "[S]till, though it issued from so rude a mouth, a mere hole in the earth, muddy too, matted with root fibres and tangled grasses, still the old bubbling burbling song, soaking through the knotted roots of infinite ages, and skeletons and treasure, streamed away in rivulets over the pavement and all along the Marylebone Road, and down towards Euston, fertilizing, leaving a damp stain" (91). The woman who owns this primeval mouth, though half-blind, crippled, and probably drunk or crazed, is none of Peter's omnipotent or servile abstractions. She accosts him and says, "[G]ive me your hand and let me press it gently . . . and if someone should see, what matter they?" While her song rises cheerfully, almost gaily, in an "invincible thread of sound" above the cottage chimneys and beech tree leaves, the woman herself remains earthbound and demands a physical contact. What this remarkable invention signifies is, of course, the life spirit itself, asking us to confront our deepest selves and memories and to play out our parts to the end. Hillis Miller has identified the song as Richard Strauss's "*Allerseelen,*" a song about the one day of the year when all the souls may rise and confront one another openly, honestly:

> Place on the table the perfuming heather,
> Bring here the last red asters,
> And let us again speak of love,
> As once in May.

> Give me your hand, that I may secretly press it,
> And if someone sees, it's all the same to me;
> Give me but one of your sweet glances,
> As once in May.

> It is blooming and breathing perfume today on every grave,
> One day in the year is free to the dead,
> Come to my heart that I may have you again,
> As once in May.[104]

One need not go as far as some feminist critics who see in the description of the rude mouth the female genitals themselves, but there is a sense of cheerful, physical fecundity in the woman and her song that was missing from the encounters of the solitary traveler. She is an embodiment of the female spirit of London, which includes the poetry of Shakespeare. In *A Room of One's Own*, Woolf asked her new women novelists to describe the unrecorded life, "the women at the street corners with their arms akimbo . . . talking with a gesticulation like the swing of Shakespeare's words; or . . . old crones stationed under doorways. . . . Above all, you must illumine your own soul with its profundities and its shallows."[105] Significantly, Richard, when he passes the old woman, senses none of her life-affirming power. He does not know "what could be done for female vagrants like that poor creature" (129).

Unfortunately, the singer is an interlude. Her fragile yet enduring song is hemmed around by the patriarchal myths of woman—first the traveler's and now Bradshaw's. This third set piece occurs after the Smiths' interview with the specialist, when Rezia has decided that he is "not a nice man" (109). "Proportion" says the narrator, is Bradshaw's "goddess" whom he worships. Proportion represses women so that they become like Lady Bradshaw, the woman who had "gone under" and "embroidered, knitted, spent four nights out of seven at home with her son" (110). As if this maintaining of the patriarchal status quo is not bad enough, Proportion has a sister harpy, the goddess Conversion. Together they are reminiscent of the figures on each side of a royal crest, and they are associated with established power. Conversion sounds very much like the first woman whom the solitary traveler met. She "bestows her blessing on those who, looking upward, catch submissively from her eyes the light of their own" (111). It is this "lady" whom Rezia has "divined." She may appear to be aristocratic, but she is a vampire concealed in Sir William's heart who comes out at night to suck dry her victims, such as Lady Bradshaw. Conversion is predatory, and Woolf links her with the more fearful side of Peter's dream by again using the word *mount:* "And then stole out from her hiding-place and mounted her throne that Goddess whose lust is to override opposition, to stamp indelibly in the sanctuaries of others the image of herself. Naked, defenceless, the exhausted, the friendless received the impress of Sir William's will. He swooped; he devoured. He shut people up" (113). Operating from within Bradshaw, Conversion has acquired male sexual powers. She mounts the naked victim, overrides, and makes her mark in the sanctuary with her seed (the image of herself). (We remember the final image of Holmes, looming over Rezia.) Conversion effectively "shuts people up," not necessarily incarcerating them (although that is Bradshaw's threat) but robbing them of a voice. The victim ends up like Peter or Septimus, friendless, with nothing to say.

Taken together, Bradshaw's twin divinities outline a grim and vicious cycle of male invention that first denies the female a full and separate identity and then ingests a single image of woman as "love, duty, self-sacrifice." This image is really a twisted and carnivorous travesty of lover, mother, and maid all in one. Enthroned, she epitomizes every well-meaning urge to aspire beyond self to group ideals. Something has gone rotten because the female has not been allowed to exist. Now the female returns in the form of a harpy to take her revenge.

Never has the battle of the sexes been more nightmarishly drawn, because in these three passages Woolf shows how men have brought their misery upon themselves. Repression of diversity results in fascism, sadism, and vampirism, with each individual a friendless, silent victim. In the context of this distorted female sexuality, and the failures represented by old and young women alike, Clarissa's ability to maintain a dignified, influential position while being sensitive to the past, to others, and to her own compromises is no mean achievement.

PETER WALSH AND SALLY SETON

Peter Walsh

Fifty-three years old (two years older than Hugh, six months older than Clarissa). Peter was "sent down" from Oxford (i.e., failed). He is a socialist whose respected Anglo-Indian family administered the affairs of a continent for three generations. He has returned to London, after five years in India (1918–23) and a failed marriage, to arrange a divorce for his lover, Daisy Simmons, who is married to a major in the Indian army and has two children.

Sally Seton

Fifty-five years old. Penniless and unhappy in her youth, she had enjoyed unconventional holidays with Clarissa at Bourton, and has become Lady Rosseter through marrying a miner's son, a bald man who owns cotton mills in Manchester. She has a garden and "five enormous boys."

Peter Walsh's name (see the Appendix) occurs far more often than Richard Dalloway's in the novel, and is second only to Clarissa's in frequency. About eleven hours of the June day are devoted to Clarissa, ten to Peter, and only three to Septimus. Sally Seton, though she appears only briefly near the end, is also named almost as often as Bradshaw. According to Nathalia Wright, there are 116 minor characters mentioned in *Mrs. Dalloway* (12 from the servant class, 36 from the bourgeoisie, 68 from the aristocracy),[106] but Peter and Sally are the most prominent representatives of "the others." They come from a social world slightly "below" Clarissa's, and beyond it as well: to the north, in Manchester, or across the sea, in India. Both characters also signify the past, particularly those heady, youthful days at Bourton, because they have loved Clarissa. *They* are the "tunnel" that Clarissa excavates during the day, and their significance is reflected in the number of times they are mentioned in the text.

Sally and Peter are in many ways soulmates. They were both to be artists, and both have failed to write. They agree on many things. They detest Hugh Whitbread, love Clarissa, and fear for the latter's conventionality. At Bourton, Sally exhorted Peter to "carry off Clarissa" and save her from being "a mere hostess" (84). They both admire the emotions, both agree that they are feeling more deeply the older they get, yet both have compromised themselves to comfort and are aware of it. Despite her conventional marriage, Sally is still more unconventional than Peter. She believes "that it was the only thing worth saying—what one felt" (212). She has no pocketknife and no repressions; she has fulfilled herself completely in motherhood and gardening. Despite "Mrs. Seton's" reappearance in *A Room of One's Own* and Woolf's warning that if she must go on having children she must do so "in twos and threes, not in tens and twelves,"[107] there is no hint that Sally is sad in Manchester. The once-rebellious girl who ran naked down the corridor at Bourton and despised the lecherous Hugh has made her peace and found her sanctuary.

The price of opting out and moving north, is, Sally feels, that Clarissa will not come to see her. The contrast between the two is cleverly suggested by the way Woolf maneuvers her characters during the party scene, for just when Clarissa and Sally have met again and are about to rekindle their friendship, they are interrupted by the arrival of the prime minister. The reader has been anticipating a long scene of catching up between the two women, to balance the scene earlier in the day with Peter, but it never comes. Symbolically, Clarissa has forsaken romantic passion for the public life of London, and while nostalgia for unfulfilled romance is acceptable between the sexes, she has censored that part of her life with Sally.

On the last page Sally declares, "What does the brain matter compared with the heart?" Yet she too is limited. One senses that for her "the heart" means the physical organ in the vegetable body rather than the finer emotions. Peter, in contrast, has continued to think throughout his life, preferring people to "cauliflowers." As a socialist he is against the establishment, and he longs for passionate human contact. The women he admires in London as physical objects disappoint him for their emotional reserve: "women don't know what passion is" (89). But now he is older, and aware of the delights of art and solitary traveling; for the dignified bachelor, society is flattering and comfortable. He concedes to the conformity of surfaces: "it had been his undoing . . . in Anglo-Indian society" (167).

Peter is there on the first page, as on the last. He is Clarissa's constant touchstone throughout the day, presumably because she knows he will be returning to London imminently. She keeps quoting his sayings, such as "I prefer men to cauliflowers." Indeed, "she owed him words: 'sentimental,' civilized'; they started up every day of her life as if he guarded her" (41). She needs his opinion as she needs his language, because with it she can interpret her world. As we might expect in a novel so suspicious of words, Clarissa's affinity for Peter goes beyond language: "they had always this queer power of communicating without words. She knew directly he criticized her" (67). Much of Clarissa's feeling for Peter is, however, nostalgia. Both of them have changed, and they do not read each other so well as at Bourton. When Peter does arrive and immediately thinks Clarissa is older (a judgment Clarissa had worried about earlier), Woolf does not record that Clarissa registers Peter's feeling at all. In fact the reserve that Peter and Clarissa have learned so well over the years makes their reunion an awkward failure.

Two other aspects get in the way. First is their egotism: before allowing full space for the other to express himself or herself, Peter and Clarissa always turn back to their own feelings of hurt or pride. She rejected his marriage proposal because she would have had to share everything and would have had no privacy. Part of that privacy was her relationship with Sally, and Clarissa recalls how her one great sexual moment with Sally was interrupted by Peter on the terrace. Her reaction of "Oh this horror!" (41) suggests that Peter's demands, as male and as intimate, will cost too much in compromise. She recalls their relationship: "Cold, heartless, a prude, he called her. Never could she understand how he cared" (10). The first assertion is clear: he accused her of being "the perfect hostess" (10) and accurately predicted her destiny, to "marry a Prime Minister and stand at the top of a staircase." But what is the sense of the phrase "how he cared"? Is she thinking of the women in India (how could he care for anyone else?), or of his *way* of caring, his demand of total involvement?

Second, what comes between them and clouds moments of unusually fine empathy is something that neither of them expresses: sexuality itself. Although both are over fifty, they inwardly react like hot-blooded young lovers. Locked now upon their chosen courses, they fitfully feel their former passion. Clarissa's behavior at the beginning of the day is that of a jilted lover. Because she has not heard from Peter, she decides to herself that "his whole life had been a failure." Her feelings are excited and contradictory, like those of a young girl in love: "he could be impossible; but adorable to walk with on a morning like this" (9). As the two sit together, both with knives drawn in defense (he holding his penknife, she her scissors), they recall that "awful summer" at Bourton. Woolf likens the process to dragging something to the surface of the lake, "something which positively hurt as it rose" (48). She sketches in the elements of a classic fight for sexual possession between father and suitor, as Peter warred with old Justin for his daughter's favor. Clarissa recalls confronting her parents with her life: she denied herself to please them, while Justin rejected the young rivals for his daughter's affection. A Freudian or fairy-tale element weaves through Woolf's prose, from the "enchanting" Peter the prince to the queen marshaling her forces (husband, daughter, setting) to "beat off the enemy" (50). In a confusion of roles the old king incestuously rejects the prince, while his daughter, locked in her high tower, takes on chivalric virtues for herself and kills the "monster" of love (50). Clarissa has one moment of wild abandon—wherein she chooses the role of neither goddess nor mother but of lover—before she resigns herself to "acting" the role of perfect party hostess, or fairy godmother in her own fairytale: "Take me with you, Clarissa thought impulsively, as if he were starting directly upon some great voyage; and then, next moment, it was as if the five acts of a play that had been very exciting and moving were now over and she had lived a lifetime in them and had run away, had lived with Peter, and it was now over" (53).

Peter is also playing sexual games. When he announces his love for Daisy he sees the concept as a sculpture in the dark, an image suggesting the forest spirit encountered by the solitary traveler. This etherealized Woman is Peter's substitute for Clarissa, and Clarissa is able to fool him into thinking she admires him for it. But, of course, "she had influenced him more than any person he had ever known"

(169). In reaction to her indifference Peter cries, and Clarissa kisses him. Her apparently lighthearted reaction—"If I had married him, this gaiety would have been mine all day!" (52)—is a shocking revelation of the sacrifice involved in the path she has chosen. Her delight now is in mothering him, and for a time he takes the role of the solitary traveler returned home from the wars. The reunion of Clarissa and Peter is altogether an amazing scene, with emotions changing like quicksilver under the pressure of ancient memories and suppressed desires.

Peter's reaction to Clarissa's rejection is to seize life in London's streets—at least, a limited form of life. He first of all identifies with the young soldiers with their marble stare, their "renunciation." Then, feeling like a young buccaneer, he pursues a woman in the crowd up Regent Street. Peter's fantasy is a violent compensation for a squandered life, but it achieves its effect, diverting him momentarily from the real (Clarissa) to the imaginary (the woman) and the general (London). But later, when Peter awakes from his revery about the solitary traveler it is to the phrase "the death of the soul." He tickets Clarissa with the phrase, recalling at Bourton her prudish rejection of a woman pregnant before marriage. His audience with Clarissa has also, however, recalled to us and to him the death of his own soul. He thinks of Elizabeth, symbol of his rival Richard's hold over Clarissa, the child Clarissa has had who would always come "before" any serious relationship between himself and Clarissa.

Peter is in many ways like Clarissa, and as we understand what really attracted him to her, we begin to understand what attracts Woolf to Clarissa's attitude toward life. Peter's relationship with Clarissa was never simply sexual. He recalls the summer when Clarissa rejected him, and we see that part of the attraction she had for him even then was not as lover but as "goddess-hostess." She may have been "wooden" (68) and Peter "cut out of wood" (69) like the figures in an enchanted castle, but there was an undeniable serenity about her polite society to which even Peter responded, especially when Clarissa invited him to join the boating party. (Indeed at the party itself Peter enjoys observing that Clarissa's "woodenness" has been "warmed through now" [192].) This happiest moment in Peter's life was insulated against passion because of his "revelation" that Clarissa was falling in love with Dalloway. This insulation is symbolized in the setting, a boat trip across the surface of the lake but not down into it. Then, as now, Peter relished that "safety."

The cost of that carefully bounded tranquility is felt in the scene of their breakup. When Peter interrupted Sally and Clarissa at Bourton, Clarissa had felt "it was like running one's face against a granite wall in the darkness" (41). Yet during their final conversation by the fountain, Clarissa herself signified a different kind of hardness, "like iron, like flint," petrified into one of the statues ornamenting the fountain itself. Against it Peter "grinds"—a sexual image used here precisely for its asexual frigidity. Clarissa's hardness is the result not of passionate jealousy but of carefully chosen decorum, a commitment to surfaces, to formal gardens and fountains rather than to the depths of that dark lake. Both characters are aware of the sterility of civility as well as its attractions.

It seems that at Bourton, Peter and Clarissa were perfectly matched in their attitudes toward manners and morals. Peter's fondness for self-analysis and Clarissa's prudery were differences only in degree. Yet despite their difficulties in communication, a tragic sense of missed opportunity prevails. Clarissa, Peter admits, "had influenced him more than any person he had ever known" (169). Years later, in the tranquility following confrontation, Peter likens the present to the surface and memories to flowers that open out revealing depths, but the present has been sapped and washed out by the past. Peter gets on with everybody now because he is androgynous: "he was not altogether manly. . . . He was a man . . . the perfect gentleman. . . . [H]e could not keep out of smoking-rooms, liked colonels, liked golf, liked bridge, and above all women's society" (173–75). Woolf suggests that only with Clarissa could Peter have functioned fully as a sexual being, and the same applies to Clarissa. They would have brought out the best in each other's sexuality, but they have chosen instead a sterile, sociable, chameleonlike sexual identity.

Peter's performance at dinner and as he walks toward Clarissa's party is an example of his expert role-playing, at once a celebration and a mockery of surfaces. All day Peter has been noticing the changes in London—in architecture, manners, dress, sexual relations—and he has been glorying in them. He feels the new generation is free from that "pyramidal accumulation which in his youth had seemed immovable" (179), the hierarchies of status and power, the sexual stereotyping that left women like pressed flowers. But at dinner he is genuinely thrilled by the Morris family's company, his worldly knowledge of "Bartlett pears," and the prospect of gossip at the Dalloways. The scene at the hotel dinner table recalls the third of the solitary traveler's visions, that of the servant clearing the table. There, one felt a painful solitude, but now Peter feels bonhomie. He too has "gone under." His failure of nerve is symbolized in his last gesture before he enters the party. He opens "the big blade of his pocket-knife" (182) not to cut through the surface to the vital depth that once pulsed but to "parry" the lances and bayonets of those figures from the past.

At the party Sally loosens Peter's tongue. He admits that he had loved Clarissa and that her refusal had spoiled his life. But is he being completely honest? He has just admitted, "I do not know what I feel," and yet on the next page we read, "We know everything, he said; at least he did" (213). We are therefore well prepared for his ambivalent reaction to Clarissa's reappearance at the party, his terror and ecstasy. Older now, and hopelessly part of that chauvinist system which meant women would always be a mystery to him, he quite likes the prospect of Clarissa as sparkling surface only. "There" is much safer than "here." Yet along with this ecstasy goes another emotion: the "terror" Peter feels at the idea that Clarissa has become "Mrs. Dalloway," that Sally has become "Lady Rosseter," and that he himself, who began the day weeping over his lost love Clarissa, is now politely chatting with her in elegant evening attire.

T. S. Eliot's "Love Song of J. Alfred Prufrock" haunts these last scenes. Not the evening sky but Septimus is laid out on the table, and not Prufrock but Peter must make his visit. As the reader emerges from the world of the novel like a party guest leaving the warm glow of companionship and conversation to enter the chill night air, everything is cruelly reversed. Gone are the dissolving resonances that softened the blow of the hour. We are left with the tolling bell that marks the passing of time, missed opportunity, and oblivion. Whatever the risks, something else must be done with our lives or we risk being enchanted, like Peter, into the living death of Clarissa's embrace:

> We have lingered in the chambers of the sea
> By sea-girls wreathed with seaweed red and brown
> Till human voices wake us, and we drown.

Conclusion

The process of reading *Mrs. Dalloway* has been one of fragmentation and dislocation, so that Peter's terror at the end is the same kind of terror that the reader has felt intermittently throughout the book. This terrified vision of society as inhuman has been built up even more frantically since Septimus's death, until the final moments when we are forced to see Clarissa from the outside, across the room—the perfect party hostess. Can she possibly bring her insights of fulfillment and completion from the little room into our world, as she tries to bring them into her party, or has she too "gone under"? Can we take that precious sense of the individual's consciousness with us, from the novel back into our own busy social world?

Our reaction to the novel's ideas finally depends on how we read Clarissa's behavior during the party. Here the novel teeters between revolution and capitulation. The bayonets and lances that have been raised all over London throughout the day remain poised. Is Clarissa endorsing the system by going back to the party? Or is she trying in the best way she can, given her position, to influence those important guests so that they will allow others their space, as she allows Richard his, Peter his, or Sally hers? Is she "parrying" the privileged, judgmental attitude she learned from her father, Justin Parry, and exhibited at Bourton, or is she perpetuating it and "parrying" instead the fundamental challenge posed by Septimus?

In considering Clarissa standing there as hostess—not at the head of the stairs martyred to her stake (Peter's image) but coming in from the smaller room (her space) and armed for personal engagement—the reader is situated precisely at the point where Woolf's debate pivots, between judgment and endorsement. Woolf balances so finely her own love and anger for the society in which she lived that we may find it impossible to choose between admiring Clarissa's civility and condemning her suppressions. Readers should trust their own response to the world of the novel, Woolf suggests: "Given time and liberty to frame his own opinion [the reader] is eventually an infallible judge."[1] But in her introduction Woolf also argued that *Mrs. Dalloway* is not a *roman à thèse* written to criticize society and to illustrate how civilization forces people to become schizophrenic. In the finished novel Septimus and Clarissa are distinct individuals, yet they are united by common human concerns. Woolf's method of writing suggests the continuity that flows beneath the outward, public incidents of urban life, although she felt that the method should not obtrude at the expense of the "rounded" (to use E. M. Forster's term) characterization: "the more successful the method, the less it attracts attention," she said. By mapping various streams of consciousness, the book enacts what Clarissa only attempts. Her sacrifices have made her too "tinselly" while Peter is seduced by Conversion and Septimus is allowed no space between triviality and Conversion. But like the wide riverbed of civilization in which Woolf believed so strongly, the book accommodates these various streams and finds in eclecticism an antidote for Bloom's "nihilism." Clarissa understands the importance of this variety, at least in theory. When she retreats from the party to the little room that symbolizes her own private space, Clarissa makes an imaginative connection between the old woman opposite her and Septimus. All three of them—herself, the old woman, and Septimus—have at least been true to their own private space; they have "found" themselves and know where their private room is. While community is important, what must be preserved within that community is the individual's right to interpret and to *read* for himself and herself. Clarissa calls this "the privacy of the soul" and thinks "Somehow one respected that—that old woman looking out of the window, quite unconscious that she was being watched" (140). Clarissa's respect for individuality is apparent throughout the novel. At the beginning of Clarissa's day we are told that "she would not say of herself, I am this, I am that" (11). She does try not to judge others. She prefers people to be different, individual, nonconformist. One of the few judgments she makes during the day is against Miss Kilman for demanding sameness, yet at the party Clarissa rejects her so-called friends and embraces the idea of her enemy Miss Kilman. Miss Kilman is eccentric and individual in her fanaticism; therefore Clarissa loves her as well as hates her—or, as Woolf puts it, "She hated her: she loved her. It was enemies one wanted, not friends. . . . They must find her if they wanted her. She was for the party" (193). What Clarissa and the narrator celebrate are the differences within the web of life. Even if Clarissa does not quite live out this ideal, it is the message of the novel.

An important corollary of this view is that social change must always be at a personal level first and must never subsume individuality in expediency. We must live in society as free individuals, and if things are to be changed we must change them by individual example rather than by coercion or legislation. At the end of *A Room of One's Own* Woolf repeated the message of *Mrs. Dalloway* more forthrightly, cautioning her female audience, "Do not dream of influencing other people. . . . Think of things in themselves."[2]

Mrs. Dalloway is therefore not simply of sociological and historical interest; it is a novel that both theorizes and enacts the political responsibilities of living in society. It speaks to our present war readiness (in the public sphere) and our war between the sexes (in the private sphere). It locates the heart of the problem in subjective perception and shows how difficult it is to live in society and at the same time to remain tolerant of other points of view. We are born into imperfect societies, already mutated in domestic life and public organization by an unhealthy division of these public and private spheres. *Mrs. Dalloway,* from its title to its final line, demands that we remove this unhealthy division by 'clari–fying' our private needs and then making space in public life for the free play of emotion.

Appendix:
Concordance to Mrs. Dalloway

Word Counts

Big Ben	8
bird(s) (bird-cage, birdlike)	20
Bourton	29
death (dead)	61
down	149
England (English, Englishman/Englishwoman)	40
fall(s) (fallen, falling)	43
fear(s) (feared)	19
"Fear no more"	8
flower(s)	58
garden(s) (gardener)	24
horror	7
India	25
life	100
mad	10
miracle(s)	9
moment(s) (momentary)	70
old	148
park	38
party	57
plunge(d) (plunging)	7
railing(s)	7
rising and falling	3
room	66
said	411
Shakespeare	20
solemn(ly) (solemnity)	12

Appendix

street	71
thought	253
time	92
war	25
young	61

Proper Names

Clarissa	246
Mrs. Dalloway	28
Clarissa Dalloway	18
Mrs. Richard Dalloway	1
Total	293

Richard	81
Richard Dalloway	21
Dalloway	20
Mr. Dalloway	11
Total	133

Peter (Peter Walsh, Mr. Walsh)	172
The Bradshaws (Sir William and Lady)	80
Sally (Sally Seton)	79
Hugh (Whitbread)	78
Septimus (Warren Smith)	76
Elizabeth (Elizabeth Dalloway)	75
Doris Kilman (Miss Kilman)	67
Lady Millicent Bruton	64
Dr. Holmes	63
Lucrezia (Rezia Warren Smith)	31
The Prime Minister	29
The Dalloways	10
The Smiths	2

Notes and References

1. Bloomsbury, War, and Modernism

1. Virginia Woolf, "Heard on the Downs: the Genesis of Myth," in *The Essays of Virginia Woolf*, vol. 2, ed. Andrew McNeillie (London: Hogarth, 1987), 40.

2. Ibid., 41.

3. *The Diary of Virginia Woolf*, vol. 1, 1915–19, ed. A. O. Bell (1977; reprint, Harmondsworth, England: Penguin, 1979), 123.

4. Ibid., 186.

5. Ibid., 293–94.

6. E. J. Leed, *No Man's Land* (Cambridge, England: Cambridge University Press, 1979), 207.

7. Ibid., 201.

8. Sandra M. Gilbert, "Soldier's Heart: Literary Men, Literary Women, and the Great War," *Signs* 8 (1982–83): 436.

9. Noreen Branson, *Britain in the Nineteen Twenties* (London: Wiedenfeld & Nicolson, 1975), 97–98.

10. A review of Elinor Mordaunt's *Before Midnight*, in *The Essays of Virginia Woolf*, vol. 2, ed. Andrew McNeillie (London: Hogarth, 1987), 7.

11. Jean Guiguet, *Virginia Woolf and her Works* (London: Hogarth, 1965), 247.

12. Margaret Church, "Joycean Structure in *Jacob's Room* and *Mrs. Dalloway*," *International Fiction Review* 4 (1977): 108.

2. The Importance of the Work

1. Malcolm Bradbury, *The Modern World: Ten Great Writers* (London: Secker & Warburg, 1988), 250.

2. *A Room of One's Own* (Harmondsworth, England: Penguin, 1945), 74.

3. Harvena Richter, "The *Ulysses* Connection: Clarissa Dalloway's Bloomsday," *Studies in the Novel* 21 (Fall 1989): 309, 313–14.

3. Critical Reception

1. Review of *Mrs. Dalloway*, in *Virginia Woolf: The Critical Heritage*, ed. Robin Majumdar and Allen McLaurin (London: Routledge & Kegan Paul, 1975), 158. Future page references in the text are to this collection.

2. Howard Harper, *Between Language and Silence: The Novels of Virginia Woolf* (Baton Rouge: Louisiana State University Press, 1982), 127.

3. A. D. Moody, *Virginia Woolf* (London and Edinburgh: Oliver & Boyd, 1963), 28.

4. Hermione Lee, *The Novels of Virginia Woolf* (London: Methuen, 1977), 93.

5. Allen McLaurin, "The Symbolic Keyboard': *Mrs. Dalloway*," in *Virginia Woolf's "Mrs. Dalloway*," ed. Harold Bloom (New York: Chelsea House, 1988), 5–14.

6. Maria DiBattista, "Virginia Woolf's Memento Mori," in Bloom, 65.

7. J. Hillis Miller, "Repetition as the Raising of the Dead," in Bloom, 81.

8. Ibid., 85, 89.

9. Perry Meisel, "Virginia Woolf and Walter Pater: Selfhood and the Common Life," in Bloom, 74.

10. Susan Squier, *Virginia Woolf and London: The Sexual Politics of the City* (Chapel Hill and London: University of North Carolina Press, 1985), 98.

11. Ibid., 115.

12. Bloom, 4.

13. Ellen Rosenman, *The Invisible Presence: Virginia Woolf and the Mother–Daughter Relationship* (Baton Rouge: Louisiana State University Press, 1986), 87.

14. Elizabeth Abel, "Narrative Structure(s) and Female Development: The Case of *Mrs. Dalloway*," in Bloom, 108–9.

15. Jeremy Hawthorn, *Virginia Woolf's "Mrs. Dalloway": A Study in Alienation* (Sussex: Sussex University Press, 1975), 10.

16. Ibid., 89.

17. Ibid., 92.

18. C. P. Snow, "Story-tellers of the Atomic Age," *New York Times,* 30 January 1955, 28–29.

4. Composition

1. Olive Anderson, *Suicide in Victorian and Edwardian England* (Oxford: Clarendon Press, 1987), 413.

2. Stephen Trombley, *"All That Summer She Was Mad"* (London: Junction, 1981), 97.

3. Lyndall Gordon, *Virginia Woolf: A Writer's Life* (London: Oxford University Press, 1984), 64.

4. *The Flight of the Mind: The Letters of Virginia Woolf,* vol. 1, 1888–1912, ed. Nigel Nicolson and Joanne Trautmann (London: Chatto & Windus, 1975), 440.

5. Trombley, *"All That Summer,"* 249–57.

6. *A Change of Perspective: The Letters of Virginia Woolf,* vol. 3, 1923–28, ed. Nigel Nicolson and Joanne Trautmann (London: Chatto & Windus, 1977), 93.

7. Lytton Strachey, *Eminent Victorians* (1918; reprint, Harmondsworth, England: Penguin, 1973), 9.

8. *The Diary of Virginia Woolf,* vol. 1, 291.

9. E. M. Forster, "Notes on the English Character," in *Abinger Harvest* (1936; reprint, Harmondsworth, England: Penguin, 1967), 15.

10. *Jacob's Room* (1922; reprint, London: Hogarth, 1945), 68. Future page references in the text are to this edition.

11. *The Question of Things Happening: The Letters of Virginia Woolf,* vol. 2, 1912–22, ed. Nigel Nicolson and Joanne Trautmann (London: Chatto & Windus, 1976), 521.

12. Susan Dick, *The Complete Shorter Fiction of Virginia Woolf* (London: Hogarth, 1987), 146.

13. Ibid., 152.

14. Ibid., 151.

15. Ibid., 153.

16. *Mrs. Dalloway's Party,* ed. Stella McNichol (London: Hogarth, 1973), 68.

17. Ibid., 70.

18. *The Diary of Virginia Woolf,* vol. 2, 1920–24, ed. A. O. Bell (1978; reprint, Harmondsworth, England: Penguin, 1981), 189.

19. J. E. Latham, "The Model for Clarissa Dalloway—Kitty Maxse," *Notes & Queries*, 214 (n.s. 16) (July 1969): 263.

20. *A Change of Perspective: The Letters of Virginia Woolf*, vol. 3, 195. Letter to Philip Morrell dated 27 July 1925.

21. Dick, *Complete Shorter Fiction*, 3.

22. Ibid., 207–8.

23. C. G. Hoffmann, "From Short Story to Novel: the Manuscript Revisions of Virginia Woolf's *Mrs. Dalloway*," *Modern Fiction Studies* 14 (1968): 174.

24. Dick, *Complete Shorter Fiction*, 177.

25. Ibid., 176.

26. Ibid., 181.

27. Ibid., 174–75.

28. Ibid., 181.

29. *The Diary of Virginia Woolf*, vol. 2, 244.

30. Ibid., 248–49.

31. Hoffmann, "From Short Story to Novel," 178.

32. *The Diary of Virginia Woolf*, vol. 2, 263.

33. Ibid., 272.

34. Ibid., 298–99.

35. Ibid., 301.

36. Ibid., 310.

37. Ibid., 312.

38. Ibid., 316.

39. Ibid., 321–23.

40. Ibid., 323.

5. Style

1. *The Common Reader* (New York: Harcourt, Brace & World, 1925), 154.

2. *Collected Essays*, vol. 1, ed. Leonard Woolf (London: Chatto & Windus, 1966), 320.

3. Ibid., 321.

4. Ibid., 324.

5. Ibid., 84.

6. Mark Hussey, *The Singing of the Real World* (Columbus: Ohio State University Press, 1986), 55. Hussey quotes Woolf's diary entry for 15 June 1929.

7. R. Humphrey, *Stream of Consciousness in the Modern Novel* (Berkeley: University of California Press, 1955), 2.

8. Dorrit Cohn, *Transparent Minds* (Princeton, N.J.: Princeton University Press, 1978), 44.

9. Ann Banfield, *Unspeakable Sentences* (Boston and London: Routledge & Kegan Paul, 1982), 292.

10. Ibid., 66–67 and passim.

11. Ibid., 52.

12. Barbara Hardy, "Love and Sympathy in Virginia Woolf," in *The Uses of Fiction,* ed. D. Jefferson and G. Martin (Milton Keynes: Open University Press, 1982), 206.

13. Ibid., 85.

14. Norman Page, *Speech in the English Novel,* 2d ed. (London: Macmillan, 1988), 44.

15. David Daiches, *Virginia Woolf* (New York: New Directions, 1942), 71.

16. Ibid., 32.

17. Humphrey, *Stream of Consciousness,* 71. See also Daiches, *Virginia Woolf.*

18. Humphrey, *Stream of Consciousness,* 70.

19. Stuart Rosenberg, "The Match in the Crocus: Obtrusive Art in Virginia Woolf's *Mrs. Dalloway,*" *Modern Fiction Studies* 13 (1967–68): 211.

20. Francis Gillen, " 'I Am This, I Am That': Shifting Distance and Movement in *Mrs. Dalloway,*" *Studies in the Novel* 4, 3 (Fall 1972): 492.

21. Geoffrey Hartman, "Virginia's Web," *Chicago Review* 14, no. 4 (Spring 1961): 25.

22. E. M. Forster, *Two Cheers for Democracy* (London: Edward Arnold, 1951), 255.

23. Morris Philipson, "Mrs. Dalloway, 'What's the Sense of Your Parties?' " *Critical Inquiry* 1 (September 1974): 124–25.

24. Ibid., 130.

25. R. A. Brower, *The Fields of Light* (New York: Oxford University Press, 1951), 128.

26. J. Hillis Miller, *Fiction and Repetition* (Oxford: Basil Blackwell, 1982), 85.

27. Makiko Minow-Pinkney, *Virginia Woolf and the Problem of the Subject* (Brighton, England: Harvester, 1987), 83.

Notes and References

28. Maria DiBattista, *Virginia Woolf's Major Novels* (New Haven, Conn., and London: Yale University Press, 1980), 26.

29. Hussey, *Singing of the Real World*, 29.

30. David Dowling, *Bloomsbury Aesthetics and the Novels of Forster And Woolf* (London: Macmillan, 1985).

31. Reprinted in *Virginia Woolf*, ed. T. S. W. Lewis (New York: McGraw-Hill, 1975), 35.

32. *A Room of One's Own*, 84.

33. David Daiches, *The Novel and the Modern World* (Chicago: University of Chicago Press, 1960), 30.

34. Ibid., 217.

35. Hartman, "Virginia's Web," 24.

36. *The Question of Things Happening: The Letters of Virginia Woolf*, vol. 2, 599.

37. Quentin Bell, *Virginia Woolf: A Biography* (two volumes in one) (New York: Harcourt Brace Jovanovich, 1972 [published in Great Britain in two volumes]), 2:106–7.

38. Daiches, *The Novel and the Modern World*, 212.

39. Ibid., 205.

40. Nancy Topping Bazin, *Virginia Woolf and the Androgynous Vision* (New Brunswick, N.J.: Rutgers University Press, 1973), 115.

41. E. Hungerford, " 'My Tunnelling Process': The Method of *Mrs. Dalloway*," *Modern Fiction Studies* 3, 2 (Summer 1957): 165.

42. Ibid., 166.

43. Maria DiBattista, "Joyce, Woolf, and the Modern Mind," in *Virginia Woolf: New Critical Essays*, ed. P. Clements and I. Grundy (London and Totowa, N.J.: Vision and Barnes & Noble, 1983), 102.

44. *Collected Essays*, vol. 1, 330–31.

45. Ibid., 109.

6. Characters and Themes

1. *Moments of Being* (1976; reprint, London: Triad/Granada, 1982), 45.

2. Ibid., 45.

3. Ibid., 96.

4. Ibid., 216.

5. Bell, *Virginia Woolf*, 1: 80.

6. *Moments of Being*, 59.

7. Latham, "Model for Clarissa Dalloway," 263.

8. Jane Marcus, "The Niece of a Nun," in *Virginia Woolf: A Feminist Slant,* ed. Jane Marcus (Lincoln and London: University of Nebraska Press, 1983), 7–36.

9. *The Flight of the Mind: The Letters of Virginia Woolf,* vol. 1, 430.

10. Philipson, "Mrs. Dalloway," 133.

11. *The Diary of Virginia Woolf,* vol. 1, 111.

12. Bernard Blackstone, *Virginia Woolf* (London: Hogarth, 1949), 94.

13. David Jones, *In Parenthesis,* quoted in Paul Fussell, *The Great War and Modern Memory* (New York and London: Oxford University Press, 1975), 51.

14. Rachel Bowlby, *Virginia Woolf: Feminist Destinations* (Oxford: Basil Blackwell, 1988), 93.

15. *A Room of One's Own,* 96–97.

16. DiBattista, *Virginia Woolf's Major Novels,* 39.

17. Gillen, " 'I Am This, I Am That,' " 490.

18. Minow-Pinkney, *Virginia Woolf,* 82.

19. *A Change of Perspective: The Letters of Virginia Woolf,* vol. 3, 189. Letter dated 14 June 1925.

20. Susan R. Gorsky, *Virginia Woolf* (Boston: Twayne, 1978), 80.

21. Minow-Pinkney, *Virginia Woolf,* 80; Suzette Henke, "*Mrs. Dalloway:* The Communion of Saints," in *New Feminist Essays on Virginia Woolf,* ed. Jane Marcus (London: Macmillan, 1981), 144.

22. Leed, *No Man's Land,* 213.

23. Allen McLaurin, *Virginia Woolf* (Cambridge, England: Cambridge University Press, 1973), 157.

24. Mitchell Leaska, *The Novels of Virginia Woolf* (London: Weidenfeld & Nicolson, 1977), 115–16.

25. A. D. Moody, *Virginia Woolf* (London and Edinburgh: Oliver & Boyd, 1963), 19.

26. Emily Jensen, "Clarissa Dalloway's Respectable Suicide," in *Virginia Woolf: A Feminist Slant,* ed. Jane Marcus (Lincoln and London: University of Nebraska Press, 1983), 170.

27. *The Diary of Virginia Woolf,* vol. 3, 1925–30, ed. A. O. Bell (1980; reprint, Harmondsworth, England: Penguin, 1982), 32.

28. Suzanne Henke, "*Mrs. Dalloway:* The Communion of Saints," in *New Feminist Essays on Virginia Woolf,* ed. Jane Marcus (London: Macmillan, 1981), 126.

29. Sandra M. Gilbert and Susan Gubar, *No Man's Land: The Place of the Woman Writer in the Twentieth Century,* vol. 2, *Sexchanges* (New Haven, Conn.: Yale University Press, 1989), 317–18.

30. Quentin Bell, *Virginia Woolf: A Biography,* 1:174.

31. *The Essays of Virginia Woolf,* vol. 2, 121.

32. Ibid., 270.

33. Olive Anderson, *Suicide in Victorian and Edwardian England* (Oxford: Clarendon Press, 1987), 387.

34. J. H. van der Hoop, *Character and the Unconscious,* trans. E. Trevelyan (London: Routledge & Kegan Paul, 1923), 28.

35. Ibid., 217.

36. Elaine Showalter, *The Female Malady* (New York: Pantheon), 172.

37. R. Graves and A. Hodge, *The Long Week-end: A Social History of Great Britain, 1918–39* (London: Faber, 1941), 27.

38. T. W. Salmon, *The Care and Treatment of Mental Diseases and War Neuroses ("Shell-Shock") in the British Army* (New York, 1917). Quoted in Leed, *No Man's Land,* 167.

39. Siegfried Sassoon, "Lamentations" (1917), in *Selected Poems* (London: Heinemann, 1925), 43.

40. Ibid., 57.

41. Ibid., 74.

42. Siegfried Sassoon, *Memoirs of a Fox-hunting Man,* in *Complete Memoirs of George Sherston* (1937; reprint, London: Reprint Society, 1940), 215–16.

43. Ibid., 557.

44. Showalter, *Female Malady,* 168.

45. Ibid., 190.

46. Leed, *No Man's Land,* 189.

47. Ibid., 185.

48. Carl Jung, *Memories, Dreams, Reflections.* Quoted in Paul Fussell, *The Great War and Modern Memory* (New York and London: Oxford University Press, 1975), 113.

49. Martin Stone, "Shell-shock and the Psychologists," in *The Anatomy of Madness,* vol. 2, ed. W. F. Bynum, R. Porter, and M. Shepherd (London: Tavistock, 1985), 242–71.

50. Alex Zwerdling, *Virginia Woolf and the Real World* (Berkeley: University of California Press, 1986), 30.

51. *Roger Fry* (London: Hogarth, 1940), 200.

52. Stone, "Shell-shock," 244.

53. Sigmund Freud, "Introduction to *Psychoanalysis and the War Neuroses*" (1919), vol. 17 of *The Standard Edition of the Complete Psychological Works of Sigmund Freud,* ed. James Strachey (London: Hogarth, 1955), 209–10.

54. Ernest Jones, *Sigmund Freud: Life and Work,* vol. 2 (London: Hogarth, 1958), 285.

55. Stone, "Shell-shock," 245.

56. Richard Aldington, *Death of a Hero* (London: Chatto & Windus, 1929), 155.

57. Leed, *No Man's Land,* 3.

58. Showalter, *Female Malady,* 171.

59. Sigmund Freud, *Group Psychology and the Analysis of the Ego* (London: Hogarth, 1922), 124.

60. Showalter, *Female Malady,* 174.

61. Virginia Woolf's notebook, quoted in Zwerdling, *Virginia Woolf and the Real World,* 131.

62. Blackstone, *Virginia Woolf,* 98.

63. Leaska, *Novels of Virginia Woolf,* 111.

64. Dowling, *Bloomsbury Aesthetics,* 140.

65. *A Room of One's Own,* 28.

66. *The London Scene* (London: Hogarth, 1975), 16.

67. Ibid., 35–36.

68. Ibid., 44.

69. *The Diary of Virginia Woolf,* vol. 1, 217–18.

70. John Stevenson, *British Society, 1914–15* (London: Allen Lane, 1984), 350.

71. Zwerdling, *Virginia Woolf and the Real World,* 121.

72. *The Diary of Virginia Woolf,* vol. 1, 151.

73. Ibid., 221.

74. Ibid., 204.

75. *Moments of Being,* 154.

76. *The Voyage Out* (1915; reprint, London: Hogarth, 1957), 38. Future page references in the text are to this edition.

77. Stephen Trombley links Dalloway's assault specifically to the abuse Virginia received in her youth from her half-brother George Duckworth (Trombley, *"All That Summer She Was Mad,"* 18).

78. *A Room of One's Own,* 86.

79. Terry Eagleton, *Exiles and Emigrés* (London: Chatto & Windus, 1970), 35.

80. Ibid., 37.

81. Jeremy Hawthorn, *Virginia Woolf's "Mrs. Dalloway": A Study in Alienation* (London: Sussex University Press, 1975), 93, 99.

82. Ibid., 105.

83. Leed, *No Man's Land,* 91.

84. *A Room of One's Own,* 56–57.

85. Leed, *No Man's Land,* 45.

86. Graves and Hodge, *Long Week-end,* 45.

87. Brian Harrison, *Separate Spheres* (London: Croom Helm, 1978), 234.

88. Sheila Jeffreys, *The Spinster and Her Enemies* (London: Pandora, 1985), 185.

89. Graves and Hodge, *Long Week-end,* 103.

90. *The Diary of Virginia Woolf,* vol. 3, 6.

91. Maria DiBattista, "Joyce, Woolf, and the Modern Mind," 109.

92. O. P. Sharma, "Feminism as Aesthetic Vision: A Study of Virginia Woolf's *Mrs. Dalloway,*" *Women's Studies* 3 (1975): 70.

93. *French Feminist Thought: A Reader,* ed. Toril Moi (London: Basil Blackwell, 1987), 116.

94. Bowlby, *Virginia Woolf,* 97.

95. *A Room of One's Own,* 111.

96. Elizabeth Abel, "Narrative Structure(s) and Female Development: The Case of *Mrs. Dalloway,*" in *The Voyage In: Fictions of Female Development,* ed. E. Abel, M. Hirsch, and E. Langland (Hanover, N.H.: University Press of New England, 1983), 161.

97. Ibid., 166.

98. Ibid., 178.

99. Ibid., 179.

100. Bowlby, *Virginia Woolf,* 184.

101. Julia Carlson, "The Solitary Traveller in *Mrs. Dalloway,*" in *Virginia Woolf,* ed. T. S. W. Lewis (New York: McGraw-Hill, 1975), 56–62.

102. Annie Leclerc, "Parole de Femme," in *French Feminist Thought: A Reader,* ed. Toril Moi (London: Basil Blackwell, 1987), 77.

103. Gilbert and Gubar, *No Man's Land,* 288.

104. Miller, *Fiction and Repetition,* 190.

105. *A Room of One's Own,* 89.

106. Nathalia Wright, "*Mrs. Dalloway*: A Study in Composition," *College English* 5, no. 7 (April 1944): 352.

107. *A Room of One's Own,* 111.

Conclusion

1. Introduction to the American Modern Library edition (1928), in *Virginia Woolf,* ed. T. S. W. Lewis (New York: McGraw-Hill, 1975), 36–37.

2. Ibid., 109.

Selected Bibliography

Text

Stella McNichol's assemblage of short stories ("Mrs. Dalloway's Party" and other stories of the "party consciousness") in *Mrs. Dalloway's Party* (London: Hogarth, 1973) gives the germ and milieu of the novel. C. G. Hoffmann, in "From Short Story to Novel: The Manuscript Revisions of Virginia Woolf's *Mrs. Dalloway*" (*Modern Fiction Studies* 14 [Summer 1966]: 171–86), takes us into the intricacies of creation. The manuscript of the novel can be seen on microfilm in *The Virginia Woolf Manuscripts from the Monk's House Papers at the University of Sussex* (Brighton, England: Harvester Press Microform Publications, 1985). There is also *A Concordance to Mrs. Dalloway by Virginia Woolf,* by J. M. Haule and P. H. Smith (London: Oxford Microform Publications, 1984), comprising a book and seven microfiches.

Biography

For the life of Virginia Woolf, one should begin with Quentin Bell's two-volume biography *Virginia Woolf* (London: Hogarth, 1972; published in the United States by Harcourt Brace Jovanovich in one volume). Biographies focusing on Woolf's madness include Roger Poole's *The Unknown Virginia Woolf* (Cambridge, England: Cambridge University Press, 1978) and Stephen Trombley's *"All That Summer She Was Mad"* (London: Junction, 1981). John Lehman's *Virginia Woolf and her World* (London: Thames & Hudson, 1975) is an illustated biography, and Quentin Bell's *Bloomsbury* (London: Weidenfeld & Nicolson, 1968; new edition, 1986) is a well-illustrated, short introduction to the Bloomsbury group.

Book-length Study

Hawthorn, Jeremy. *Virginia Woolf's "Mrs Dalloway": A Study in Alienation.* Sussex: Sussex University Press, 1975. Emphasizes the dualistic tensions in the novel, arising from Woolf's own class-bound background and a deep sense of the alienation of the modern city.

Essay Collections

Beja, Morris, ed. *Critical Essays on Virginia Woolf.* Boston: G. K. Hall, 1985. Contains the review by Hughes and articles by Miller and Zwerdling.

Bloom, Harold, ed. *Modern Critical Interpretations of Virginia Woolf's "Mrs. Dalloway."* New York: Chelsea House, 1988. An excellent collection that contains many of the important articles listed in this bibliography, including ones by McLaurin, Lee, DiBattista, Meisel, Miller, Abel, Ruotolo, and Zwerdling.

Bloom, Harold, ed. *Modern Critical Views of Virginia Woolf.* New York: Chelsea House, 1986. Contains articles on *Mrs. Dalloway* by Abel, Brower, Hartman, and Miller.

Parts of Books and Articles

Abel, Elizabeth. "Narrative Structures and Female Development: The Case of *Mrs. Dalloway.*" In *The Voyage In: Fictions of Female Development,* edited by E. Abel, M. Hirsch, and E. Langland, 161–85. Hanover, N.H.: University Press of New England, 1983.

Alexander, Jean. *The Venture of Form in the Novels of Virginia Woolf,* 85–104. Port Washington, N.Y.: Kennikat, 1974. Woolf is antipower, procivilization: "What is left is a harmonious movement of contrary individuals within a ceremonious form, dependent nevertheless on a solitary imperative of choice."

Apter, T. E. *Virginia Woolf: A Study of her Novels,* 50–72. New York: New York University Press, 1979.

Bazin, Nancy Topping. *Virginia Woolf and the Androgynous Vision,* 102–23. New Brunswick, N.J.: Rutgers University Press, 1973.

Beja, Morris. "The London of Mrs. Dalloway." *Virginia Woolf Miscellany* 7 (Spring 1977): 4. A useful, one-page map of London that shows the location of the main events in the novel.

Selected Bibliography

Beker, M. "London as a Principle of Structure in *Mrs. Dalloway*." *Modern Fiction Studies* 18 (1972): 375–85.

Bowlby, Rachel. *Virginia Woolf: Feminist Destinations*, 80–98. Oxford: Basil Blackwell, 1988. A chapter entitled "Thinking Forward through Mrs. Dalloway's Daughter" considers Clarissa's sacrifices and Elizabeth's suitability as a feminist of the new generation.

Brower, Reuben. *The Fields of Light*, 123–37. New York: Oxford University Press, 1951. This early study stresses the Shakespearean unity of Woolf's imagination through metaphor and symbol, as well as discussing references to the plays.

Daiches, David. *Virginia Woolf*. Rev. edition. New York: New Directions, 1963. A clear exposition of Woolf's style, along with criticism of her lack of "a certain necessary vitality."

DiBattista, Maria. "Joyce, Woolf, and the Modern Mind." In *Virginia Woolf: New Critical Essays*, edited by P. Clements and I. Grundy, 102–9. London and Totowa, N.J.: Vision and Barnes & Noble, 1983.

———. *Virginia Woolf's Major Novels: The Fables of Anon*, 22–63. New Haven, Conn., and London: Yale University Press, 1980. A chapter entitled "Virginia Woolf's Memento Mori" discusses the interactions of time and space and concludes that Virginia Woolf's purpose is to "inaugurate, in the time of the novel, the reign of the feminine law-giver."

Dowling, David. *Bloomsbury Aesthetics and the Novels of Forster and Woolf*, 136–48. London: Macmillan, 1985. Examines the connections between painting and aesthetic form, and applies these ideas to the shape of the novel.

Ebert, Teresa L. "Metaphor, Metonymy, and Ideology: Language and Perception in *Mrs. Dalloway*." *Language and Style* 182, (Spring 1985): 152–64.

Edwards, Lee R. "Wars and Roses: The Politics of *Mrs. Dalloway*." In *The Authority of Experience: Essays in Feminist Criticism*, edited by A. Diamond and L. Edwards, 160–77. Amherst: University of Massachusetts Press, 1977. An autobiographical approach that begins with some critics' anger at Clarissa's position and moves to an understanding of the validity of the hostess role in keeping matters personal and avoiding the dangerous abstractions of politics.

Fleishman, Avrom. *Virginia Woolf: A Critical Reading*, 69–95. Baltimore, Md., and London: Johns Hopkins University Press, 1975. Analyzes the system of symbolism in the novel and closely reads the final scene as an example of dramatic *anagnorisis*.

Fraser, June. "*Mrs. Dalloway*: Virginia Woolf's Greek Novel." *Research Studies* 47 (1979):221–28.

Gillen, Francis. " 'I Am This, I Am That': Shifting Distance and Movement in *Mrs. Dalloway*." *Studies in the Novel* 4, 3 (Fall 1972): 484–93. A sensitive reader-response approach that likens the reader's experience to Clarissa's, as one of oscillation and discovery.

Guiguet, Jean. *Virginia Woolf and Her Works.* London: Hogarth, 1965. Argues that *Mrs. Dalloway* is the most Proustian of Virginia Woolf's novels.

Guth, Deborah. " 'What a Lark! What a Plunge!': Fiction as Self-Evasion in *Mrs. Dalloway.*" *Modern Language Review* 84, pt. 1(January 1989): 18–25. Clarissa never plunges, that is, commits herself to life, and Woolf is an accomplice in her pretense of involvement.

Hafley, James. *The Glass Roof: Virginia Woolf as Novelist,* 60–76. Berkeley and Los Angeles: University of California Press, 1954. A useful survey of the influence of Bergson, Joyce, and Proust.

Haring-Smith, Tori. "Private and Public Consciousness in *Mrs. Dalloway* and *To the Lighthouse.*" In *Virginia Woolf: Centennial Essays,* edited by E. K. Ginsberg and L. M. Gottlieb, 143–62. Troy, N.Y.: Whitston, 1983.

Harper, Howard. *Between Language and Silence: The Novels of Virginia Woolf,* 109–34. Baton Rouge: Louisiana State University Press, 1982.

Hartman, Geoffrey. "Virginia's Web." *Chicago Review* 14, no. 4 (Spring 1961): 20–32.

Hasler, J. "Virginia Woolf and the Chimes of Big Ben." *English Studies* 63, 2 (April 1982): 142–58.

Henke, Suzette. "*Mrs. Dalloway:* The Communion of Saints." In *New Feminist Essays on Virginia Woolf,* edited by Jane Marcus, 125–47. Lincoln: University of Nebraska Press, 1981. Through use of Greek and Christian symbolism, Virginia Woolf mounts "a strong critique of patriarchy" and the class system.

———. " 'The Prime Minister': A Key to *Mrs. Dalloway.*" In *Virginia Woolf: Centennial Essays,* edited by E. K. Ginsberg and L. M. Gottlieb, 127–41. Troy, N.Y.: Whitston, 1983.

Hessler, J. G. "Moral Accountability in *Mrs. Dalloway.*" *Renascence* 30 (1978): 126–36.

Hussey, Mark. *The Singing of the Real World: The Philosophy of Virginia Woolf's Fiction.* Columbus: Ohio State University Press, 1986. References to *Mrs. Dalloway* are scattered throughout this excellent introduction to the philosophical preoccupations in all of Virginia Woolf's work.

Jensen, Emily. "Clarissa Dalloway's Respectable Suicide." In *Virginia Woolf: A Feminist Slant,* edited by Jane Marcus, 162–79. Lincoln: University of Nebraska Press, 1983. Clarissa's sacrifice of her life to the role of hostess is "one of the most common suicides for women." In Septimus she recognizes a similar fate.

Kelley, Alice van Buren. *The Novels of Virginia Woolf: Fact and Vision,* 88–113. Chicago: University of Chicago Press, 1973.

Selected Bibliography

Kenney, S. M., and E. J. Kenney. "Virginia Woolf and the Art of Madness." *Massachusetts Review* 23, 1 (Spring 1982): 161–85.

Leaska, Mitchell. *The Novels of Virginia Woolf: From Beginning to End*, 85–117. New York: John Jay, 1977. A sympathetic account of the themes of sexuality and marriage, and the importance of ritual in society.

Lee, Hermione. *The Novels of Virginia Woolf*, 91–115. London: Methuen, 1977. A brief biographical setting, followed by a succinct plot summary and a good discussion of the principle of time in *Mrs. Dalloway.*

McLaurin, Allen. *Virginia Woolf: The Echoes Enslaved*. Cambridge, England: Cambridge University Press, 1973. Connects the novel with Roger Fry's ideas about kinesthesia and follows the imagery of cutting and scraping.

McNichol, Stella. *Virginia Woolf and the Poetry of Fiction*, 62–90. London and New York: Routledge, 1990. Rhythm and pattern in the novel.

Miller, J. Hillis. *Fiction and Repetition: Seven English Novels*, 176–202. Cambridge, Mass.: Harvard University Press, 1982.

Minow-Pinkney, Makiko. *Virginia Woolf and the Problem of the Subject*, 54–83. Brighton, England: Harvester, 1987. Employing recent semiotic and critical theories, the author argues that the voice of the narrator is the most interesting feature of *Mrs. Dalloway,* as it tries to avoid polarizations and marginalization.

Moody, A. D. *Virginia Woolf.* London and Edinburgh: Oliver & Boyd, 1963. A clear, outspoken critique of the novel, and a useful, brief survey of Woolf's life and work.

Naremore, James. *The World without a Self: Virginia Woolf and the Novel,* 77–111. New Haven, Conn., and London: Yale University Press, 1973. The novel is elegiac in tone and finally comes to terms with death.

Panken, Shirley. *Virginia Woolf and the "Lust of Creation,"* 115–40. Albany: State University of New York, 1987. The novel is an extended mourning process regarding issues of unlived life, failed marriage, and confusion of identity, and it stresses the role and idea of the mother.

Paul, Janis. *The Victorian Heritage of Virginia Woolf,* 123–51. Norman, Okla.: Pilgrim Books, 1987. While there is a vein of concreteness in the oppressive Victorian setting of *Mrs. Dalloway,* its "unity of structure, thought and language . . . creates not limitation but communication." Clarissa "has learned that, in her time and place, she must cultivate her own garden."

Quick, J. R. "The Shattered Moment: Form and Crisis in *Mrs. Dalloway* and *Between the Acts.*" *Mosaic* 7 (Spring 1974): 127–36. The artistic resolution at the end of *Mrs. Dalloway* is grim: "death the party-crasher stands at the head of the train of little deaths that have occurred throughout Clarissa's day."

Richter, Harvena. "The Canonical Hours in *Mrs. Dalloway*." *Modern Fiction Studies* 28, 2 (Summer 1982): 236–40.

———. "The *Ulysses* Connection: Clarissa Dalloway's Bloomsday." *Studies in the Novel* 21, no. 3 (Fall 1989): 305–19. Biographic, thematic, and imagistic connections are traced between Joyce's *Ulysses* and Woolf's city novels, suggesting "a far closer relationship between the two novels than has hitherto been suspected." (305)

Rigney, Barbara H. "The Sane and the Insane: Psychosis and Mysticism in *Mrs. Dalloway*." In *Madness and Sexual Politics in the Feminist Novel*, 41–63. Madison: University of Wisconsin Press, 1978.

Rosenberg, Stuart. "The Match in the Crocus: Obtrusive Art in Virginia Woolf's *Mrs. Dalloway*." *Modern Fiction Studies* 13 (1967–78): 211–19. A rare attack on Woolf's overly controlled prose, the article identifies the right issues for debate concerning Woolf's style.

Rosenman, Ellen. *The Invisible Presence: Virginia Woolf and the Mother-Daughter Relationship*, 75–92. Baton Rouge: Louisiana State University Press, 1986. Septimus's suicide "simultaneously calls into question and affirms Clarissa's symbolic mode, revealing both the literal reality which it evades and the necessity for doing so." Clarissa survives in her femininity by seeing the world symbolically.

Rosenthal, Michael. *Virginia Woolf*, 87–102. London: Routledge & Kegan Paul, 1979. "Totally absorbed in life . . . Clarissa can finally no more be judged than can life itself." *Mrs. Dalloway* is Virginia Woolf's most personal book.

Ruotolo, Louis. *The Interrupted Moment*. Stanford: Stanford University Press, 1986. A chapter entitled "The Unguarded Moment: *Mrs. Dalloway*" gives a close analysis of the rhythms and important moments during the novel and argues positively for the ending: "She has, with Septimus, broken through to the reality of 'something not herself.' "

Schlack, Beverly Ann. "A Freudian Look at *Mrs. Dalloway*." *Literature and Psychology* 23 (1973): 49–58.

Sharma, O. P. "Feminism as Aesthetic Vision: A Study of Virginia Woolf's *Mrs. Dalloway*." *Women's Studies* 3 (1975): 61–73.

Spilka, Mark. *Virginia Woolf's Quarrel with Grieving*, 47–74. Lincoln and London: University of Nebraska Press, 1980. Spilka calls Clarissa's exultation at the news of Septimus's suicide "a psycho-literary cop-out."

Squier, Susan. *Virginia Woolf and London: The Sexual Politics of the City*, 91–121. Chapel Hill and London: University of North Carolina Press, 1985. A chapter entitled "The Carnival and Funeral of Mrs. Dalloway's London" sees the city as patriarchal and the novel as the beginning of Virginia Woolf's lifelong study of the "relationship of woman's traditional social role to the nature and structure of British society."

Selected Bibliography

Stewart, J. F. "Impressionism in the Early Novels of Virginia Woolf." *Journal of Modern Literature* 9, 2 (May 1982): 237–66.

Wright, Nathalia. "*Mrs. Dalloway:* A Study in Composition." *College English* (April 1944): 351–58. Like Richter, Wright suggests that the pattern of the hours in a single day provided the structure for the novel.

Wyatt, Jean. "*Mrs. Dalloway:* Literary Allusion as Structural Metaphor." *PMLA* 88 (1973): 440–51.

Zwerdling, Alex. *Virginia Woolf and the Real World*, 120–43. Berkeley and London: University of California Press, 1986. Traces the novel's movement through London's streets.

Index

Index

The Author

David Dowling is a New Zealander who received his doctorate from the University of Toronto. He has taught in Australia and New Zealand and is now senior lecturer at Massey University, Palmerston North, New Zealand. For many years he has taught undergraduate and graduate courses on Virginia Woolf and the Bloomsbury group, and he has published articles and books on Woolf and E. M. Forster, notably *Bloomsbury Aesthetics and the Novels of Forster and Woolf* (1985). He is also the author of *Fictions of Nuclear Disaster* (1987) and *William Faulkner* (1989) and has edited a book on British novelists, *Novelists on Novelists* (1984), and a collection of the writings of New Zealand playwright Bruce Mason. He was editor of the New Zealand literary quarterly *Landfall* for eight years.